THE
DAWN
OF MAN

THE
DAWN
OF MAN

STEVE PARKER

CONSULTANT EDITOR
PROFESSOR MICHAEL DAY

Eagle
Editions

A QUANTUM BOOK

Published by Eagle Editions
an imprint of Eagle Remainders Ltd
2A Kingsway, Royston
Hertfordshire SG8 5EG

Copyright ©1992 Quarto Publishing plc

This edition printed 1998

ISBN 1-902328-15-9

QUMDOM

This book is produced by
Quantum Books Ltd
6 Blundell Street
London N7 9BH

Printed in Singapore by
Star Standard Industries Pte Ltd

CONTENTS

INTRODUCTION

Almost every human society has its beliefs or its folk tales about how and where it originated. In some societies it may amount to a legend handed down by word of mouth, or in more complex societies it may consist of an elaborate and detailed account that is associated with a set of beliefs involving a god/creator, worship, and a code of conduct that (if adhered to) will bring resurrection after death and reunion with the creative force. An example of the former is the Masai tribe in East Africa, who believe that their people originated from an active volcano in their part of the world – a clear link between their origins and the most powerful natural force in their environment. The Christian creation myth centres on Adam and Eve in the garden of Eden, but the idyll was soon shattered by the advent of disobedience to God's will and retribution in the form of the flood. This account, originating in the Near East, had profound effects for many centuries on geological thought and the interpretation of the findings of naturalists.

A HISTORY OF OUR HISTORY

Greek and Roman scholars were well aware from antiquity of the existence of monkeys and apes, and the similarity of these animals to humans did not escape them; neither did it escape the ancient thinkers of Asia who often portrayed Hanuman, the Monkey-God, in human form and proportion. The Greek philosopher and "Father of Natural History" Aristotle (*c.*330 BC) observed the features that groups of animals share, and he created the first classification of animal types. In his great work, *Historia animalium*, he assigned animals to two groups: those with red blood, and those he thought were without blood. Broadly, the first group are what we today call the vertebrates (animals with backbones): fish, amphibians, reptiles, birds, and mammals. The second group were the invertebrates, such as worms, shellfish, and insects. In this system he placed apes between humans and monkeys, and noted that monkeys have tails while apes do not: "Some animals share the properties of man and the quadrupeds, as the ape, the monkey, and the baboon." Aristotle also wrote of a "tree of life," with humans at the top, although he was not explicit about the notion of evolution.

Heraclitus (*c.*500 BC) thought that animal species could change. Anaximander of Miletus (*c.*570 BC) was the first to propose a theory of evolution and was also the first to use the verb "to evolve" (METABIΩNAI). He concluded that humans had originated from a different animal species. Pliny, the Roman historian and cavalry officer (AD 23–79), raised the status of the apes by calling them "wild men." He suggested that humans, unlike the "birds of the air and wild beasts," had the unique ability to change the world for the worse: "It is true that the Earth brought forth poisons, but who discovered them except Man?...It is not unusual for us to poison rivers and the very elements of which the world

Adam and Eve in the Garden of Eden. Many traditional beliefs hold that humans were created by a god or divine spirit, and were specially endowed beings that stood apart from the rest of the animal world.

is made; even the air itself, in which all things live, we corrupt till it injures and destroys." However these writings were over-shadowed by the power of the great Plato and his precise view of an ordered and unchanging universe.

ADVANCES DURING THE RENAISSANCE

It was not until 15 centuries later that Renaissance thinkers challenged the conceptions of Plato, Aristotle, and the anatomist Galen. Leonardo da Vinci dissected human bodies and drew in exquisite detail what he found – he saw even more clearly the close similarities between the anatomy of humans and that of other animals. His work was extended by Andreas Vesalius in his famous book *De humani corporis fabrica*, published in 1543. Vesalius established the principles, in anatomy and biology, of recording in precise detail what is actually there.

The foundations of comparative anatomy were later built upon by Edward Tyson, who dissected a chimpanzee in 1699 and termed it *Homo sylvestris*, "man of the woods." Even before, Nicolaus Tulp, who was President of the College of Surgeons in Amsterdam and the principal subject of the famous Rembrandt painting *The Anatomy School*, had also dissected a chimpanzee and termed it a "man of the forest." The links between humans and apes were being recognised and were later enshrined by Linnaeus, the founder of our modern system of classifying and naming plants and animals.

LINNAEUS

The Swedish biologist Carolus Linnaeus (Carl von Linné), born in 1707, was eventually professor of botany and medicine at the University of Uppsala for

Charles Darwin proposed the theory of evolution by natural selection in 1859 in his momentous book On the Origin of Species. *Darwin was fully aware of the furore his proposals would create, even though he was not explicit about the origins of humans in the book. Privately, he likened his suggestion that animals (including humans) were not specially created by God, but had evolved as part of nature, to "confessing a murder."*

botany and medicine at the University of Uppsala for more than 30 years. He saw his task as bringing order to nature's bewildering diversity.

In his massive mid – 18th century classification of the natural world, *Systema Naturae*, Linnaeus classified humans and apes together in his highest category in the Mammalia, the order of Primates. He saw this grouping as the pinnacle of the animal world. He also christened living humans with the generic name *Homo*, New Latin for "Man," and the species name *sapiens*, meaning sapient, understanding or "wise." This reflected our special status.

Linnaeus" system was originally designed for living animals and plants, but it soon became obvious that it had relevance to fossils. Linnaeus found it hard to deal with these "natural stone objects" without a time frame, due to his belief in the unchanging or immutable nature of animal species.

THE EARTH

Until the late 18th century the prevailing view was that the Earth was basically volcanic in origin, and sedimentary rocks, particularly those containing fossils, were the result of catastrophes such as volcanic eruptions or the biblical flood. Such animal remains were termed *antediluvian* – from "before the deluge." This view was challenged in 1788 by the work of William Hutton, an Edinburgh doctor and scientist. He was intrigued by geological unconformities, in which rocks of strikingly different types are in direct contact and lie on top of each other. Unconformities were not readily explained by the prevailing, somewhat static, view of the time, in which the Earth was an unchanging structure awaiting yet another catastrophe. Hutton was also aware of the cycle of the evaporation of the oceans, condensation of the water vapour into clouds, followed by rainfall. He

The first fossils of Neandertal Man were found in a cave high on the slopes of the Neander Valley near Düsseldorf, Germany, in 1857. These humanlike bones became the centre of controversy two years later, when they were used both to support and deny Darwin's theory of evolution by natural selection (see Chapter Six). This photograph is dominated by the skull roof with its heavy, projecting brow ridges.

coupled this with the theory that older rocks are broken down and weathered by natural forces to form particles of sediments such as sand and mud; these are washed into the sea, settle out into marine deposits, and form hard rocks once more. Hutton stated that this dynamic process had occurred uniformly and continuously for many millennia. The principle was termed Uniformitarianism, and it was finally made widely known and understood by John Playfair in 1802 and Charles Lyell in 1838.

The realisation that stratified rocks (layers of sediments made up from the weathering of older rocks) contained fossils from a variety of levels, and therefore ages, cast serious doubts on the widely-held biblical flood or single-catastrophe explanation of fossils. The door was opening for an understanding of palaeontology, the study of the fossil remains of now-extinct animals, and an appreciation of the time intervals that have separated geological events.

FOSSILS

The first reference to fossils may be that of Xenophanes of Colophone (*c.* 540 BC). He realised that the presence of shells and fish bones in rocks was evidence that the rock layers were once under water. He had observed fossils in differing strata, and he concluded that each layer boundary represented a universal extinction of all plants and animals (including humans), followed by a recreation of the living world. This is perhaps the earliest record of a catastrophic view of geology.

In the Middle Ages fossils were found in Europe from time to time. They were often of ice-age mammoths that were interpreted as the bones of giants. The fossils were kept as curios and displayed in churches and public places. Perhaps the most famous of these discoveries was *Homo diluvii testis* – "man who had witnessed the flood." In 1726 near the village of Oeningen, Switzerland, Dr Johann Jakob Scheuchzer found a skeleton that he believed represented one of the men whose sins had brought the disaster of the deluge upon the world. (In fact the fossil skeleton is that of a salamander from millions of years ago.)

The great French naturalist Comte de Buffon was one of the first to question the biblical estimate of the age of the Earth. Archbishop Ussher of Armagh Ireland, had stated that the Earth was created by God in 4004 BC, from genealogical evidence in the Old Testament.

Baron Georges Cuvier is here pictured in later life, holding a rock containing a fossilised fish. So great was his reputation as a comparative anatomist that it was said he could predict the anatomy of an entire skele ton from one of its bones. However, he insisted that, unlike fossil reptiles and fossil fish, there were no fossil humans.

Buffon favoured an age of at least 75,000 years, to permit the "slow succession" of movements of all great works of nature. Among his pupils were Jean-Baptiste Lamarck, Geoffroy St. Hilaire, and the renowned Georges Cuvier.

Baron Georges Cuvier (1769–1832) was one of the greatest naturalists of all time. He showed that the fossil skeletons of extinct animals could be articulated (fitted back together), their anatomical characteristics could be determined and compared with living species, and their lifestyles could be reconstructed from their remains. Cuvier knew that fossils were relics of prehistoric life which had existed for thousands of years, and whose succession identified a time scale for the history of the world. But he could not bring himself to include humans in his scheme, declaring, "Fossil man does not exist." This unfortunate triumph of prejudice over reason – seen nowhere else in his work – became established dogma on the basis of his massive reputation. It was not seriously challenged until 30 years after his death, when Charles Darwin established his theory of the origin of species.

THEORIES AND THEORISTS

Ancient thinkers of Greece and Rome had considered the possibility that animals might change through time, but their suggestions were lost in the Dark Ages, to be superseded by the biblical story of the individual creation of species, and its consequence of their immutability. But increasing knowledge of comparative anatomy and classification, coupled with the acceptance of fossils as evidence of past life, made the unchanging nature of species seem less likely. In 1802 in Paris, Buffon's pupil, Jean-Baptiste Lamarck, suggested that species cannot be distinguished completely from each other. Some seven years later he observed: "Everything undergoes in time the most gradual changes." In his view the changes were brought about by the influence of the environment on the individual, and that ultimately that creature or plant is transformed during its lifetime. The features or characteristics acquired in the course of adaptation to the environment are then passed on to later generations. Lamarckism thus explains evolution by the inheritance of acquired characteristics.

Lamarck's ideas were not accepted for two reasons. Firstly, they were flawed in terms of his explanation for the changes he postulated. The environment does not *directly* affect the inheritable characteristics (now known as genes) of an animal or plant, as he suggested. The real mechanism, which escaped Lamarck, was identified later by Darwin and Wallace. Secondly, the young Cuvier (whose reputation was immense and growing) did not accept the evolution of one species into another, and he totally rejected the application of any evolutionary theory to the case of mankind.

Charles Darwin's father was a doctor in Shrewsbury, England, and his grandfather, Erasmus Darwin, another doctor and naturalist whose views were not unlike those of Lamarck. The young Charles was selected to join a voyage on HMS *Beagle*, a Royal Navy survey ship, as the naturalist for the expedition. The voyage around South America and the Pacific lasted five years. Darwin collected a prodigious quantity of animal, plant, fossil, and geological specimens. During that period Darwin's views on the origin of species were formed by his observations of the creatures and plants of the Galapagos

Islands, a remote group some 600 miles west of Ecuador. The Galapagos animals clearly had associations with those of South America, but they were not exactly the same. It was plain that the creatures of these islands had arrived there from South America at some point in the past. In the course of time they had varied to give rise to differing, but closely related, forms.

These observations convinced Darwin that some form of evolution had taken place. He also discovered fossils of large extinct South American mammals, such as the giant sloth. It was difficult to account for them on the basis of the biblical flood, or the catastrophic theory of fossils espoused by Cuvier. Coupled with the conviction that gradual change was the mechanism of land formation (after Hutton, Playfair, and Lyell), Darwin began to view gradual change as the link between the living and the dead – the extant and the fossil. His theories still

Alfred Russel Wallace, co-author with Charles Darwin of the first scientific report concerning evolution by natural selection, published in 1858. After this, he stepped aside and allowed Darwin and his supporters to continue the work. Wallace spent many years as a professional collector of natural history specimens, especially insects, in South America and southeastern Asia.

lacked, however, a proposal for the driving force that would accelerate and direct the pattern of change.

The idea came to him after reading a book written in 1798 by the economist-clergyman Thomas Malthus. Malthus believed that unlimited human fecundity would lead to over-population and starvation as the people of the world outran their ability to produce food; he talked of a "struggle for life." Darwin extended this idea to suggest that in the struggle, some individuals with favourable variations would succeed, while others would die out. The principle of the 'survival of the fittest' as the mechanism of natural selection was born. It was simple, it accounted for the cumulative effects of a myriad of small changes over time, but it needed to be proved.

However, Darwin was not the only naturalist to be thinking along these lines. Alfred Russel Wallace, a traveller and zoologist, was a believer in evolution. In June 1858, as Darwin laboured at a book on his theory, he received a manuscript from Wallace, who had come – perhaps more intuitively – to almost identical conclusions. Darwin hastily conferred with his friends, and their advice was to present the theory under their joint names – the book would follow later. This was done by a joint paper read at a Linnean Society meeting in London in 1858, thus ensuring Wallace his due honour.

EVOLUTION AND ACCEPTANCE

Charles Darwin finally published *On the Origin of Species* in 1859. It was a massive piece of work and showed beyond doubt that evolution had taken place, basically by the mechanism of natural selection that Darwin proposed. The vexed question of the application of the theory to humans was left untouched, other than by the remark "Light will be thrown on the origin of man and his history." This telling phrase informs us not only that Darwin was well aware of the problem that he faced with Christian dogma, but also that the lack of human fossils was likely to be remedied. The publication of *On the Origin of Species* did indeed produce a furore and battles that Darwin, a sickly man, did not relish. One who did was Thomas Henry Huxley, later to be known as "Darwin's Bulldog." Huxley took on and defeated Bishop "Soapy Sam" Wilberforce in debate at the British Association meeting in Oxford, in 1860.

The bold Huxley now confronted the question of human origins, in the light of the theory of evolution

Thomas Huxley's Man's Place in Nature *ventured into areas which Darwin had only hinted at in* On the Origin of Species. *It set out clearly the evidence for the view that humans have evolved as part of nature; we were not specially created separately from the rest of the natural world. The drawings on the left compare the skeletons of living apes and the human. The smaller portraits show Huxley himself on the left, and the eminent German biologist Ernst Haeckel on the right, flanked by a "tree" of apes from his own work (see Chapter Five)*

established by Darwin. His essays, *Man's Place in Nature* (1863), set out his position on the close relationship between humans and apes. He examined some of the few fossil human remains then known, including the Neandertal skull cap found in 1856 (see page 110). Huxley also critically examined Darwin's theory, but he made it quite clear that he accepted its application to humans: "There cannot be the slightest doubt in the world that the argument which applies to the improvement of the horse from an earlier stock, or of an ape from an ape, applies to the improvement of man from some simpler and lower stock than man." Darwin then took the final step himself and in 1871 published The *Descent of Man*. In this he ventured the opinion that human origins may well have been in Africa, since our closest living animal relatives the chimps and gorillas dwell there.

THE HARD EVIDENCE

The Darwinian theory predicts that if the evolution of man from some "lower stock" actually did take place, then there should be the fossil evidence to prove the point. In 1871 only Neandertal remains were known. Opinions on their antiquity varied. Virchow, the great German pathologist, considered them to be of a "man" deformed by disease, while others thought that they belonged to a hermit. In 1898 in Java, Eugene Dubois (a Dutch anatomist, doctor, and soldier) found the first fossil human remains whose antiquity seemed assured, and whose skull anatomy, at least, seemed primitive – a

Bishop Samuel "Soapy Sam" Wilberforce, so-called for his smooth and slippery rhetoric. In 1860 Wilberforce and Thomas Huxley engaged in heated debate on the subject of human origins. Huxley condemned the bishop's sarcasm and narrow-mindedness, and his refusal to consider the mass of evidence with an open mind.

small brain, and heavy bony ridges over the eye sockets. The first so-called "missing link" had been found. There were to be many more such links from Java, China, Europe, the Near East, and Africa.

In the 1930s and 1940s, Ralph von Koenigswald added to the fossil collections in Java. At the same time Davidson Black, in association with his Chinese colleagues, discovered "Peking Man." The Far Eastern specimens represent a primitive form of human known as *Homo erectus*. Examples of the same human type were also found by the French in North Africa, and later by the Leakey family in East Africa. But where did *Homo erectus* come from, and to what did this species give rise? Neither question has a definitive answer even today, but the discovery of the Taung australopithecine ("southern ape") skull in 1924 by Raymond Dart in South Africa opened up a vista of "ape-men" from Africa, some of whom certainly preceded *Homo erectus* in time. In the 1960s Louis and Mary Leakey, at Olduvai Gorge, Tanzania, discovered fossils now named *Homo habilis*, perhaps the bridge between Dart's *Australopithecus* and *Homo erectus*. Despite all these finds, the origin of our own species has proved elusive to pinpoint.

THE APPLICATION OF SCIENCE

What has modern science to offer the paleoanthropologist of today? The commonest question for those who work with fossils is: "How do you know how old it is?" The answer has several parts. The fossil must be recovered from its deposit with care, and identified as having been laid down in that layer at the time when the layer was formed. It must be shown to be contemporaneous with the sediment in which it was found. If the fossil passes these tests, then other methods become appropriate, such as radiocarbon dating and potassium-argon dating, that depend on the decay of radioactive elements in the specimens, to give an age in years. New methods are appearing all the time, such as electron spin resonance (ESR), that help to confirm the dates by alternative means.

The age of a fossil can help to place it in the time sequence that is needed to build evolutionary trees. These devices give us some idea of the way the fossils can document the evolutionary changes that have taken place in human evolutionary history. In recent years, the usual Linnean method of classifying plants and animals has been joined by a method devised by German biologist Willi Hennig. The Linnean technique of showing affinity between animal or plant forms depends on demonstrating similar features in their anatomy. The Hennigian system looks for the first appearance of novelty; it is the sharing of this novel feature that is paramount in demonstrating affinity in this system. The graphic representation of the Hennigian conclusions are cladograms – timeless diagrams of relationships. They have no real pretensions to the identification of ancestry, but they do set out testable hypotheses for grouping and classifying living things.

The advent of molecular biology and the ability to trace genetic markers in living things is having an impact on the search for our origins. Genes change or mutate through time. If mutation rates are constant (and it is a big "if"), then the rate of change in genetic materials can be used to predict the separation point between human and primate groups, and human and human groups. This can be compared with the fossil record, and family trees constructed.

Paleoanthropology is a specialised branch of palaeontology, the study of animal life of the past. It is of particular interest because we ourselves are the animal under study. It is not an experimental science, capable of repetition. But the theories that it generates can produce predictions, which can be tested against new finds and new techniques. The results are usually interesting, sometimes startling, and always relevant to us all – members of *Homo sapiens*, today's dominant branch of a long and distinguished family tree.

Michael H Day

"Frozen behaviour": simple stone tools of the Acheulean type, often associated with fossils of an earlier group of humans, Homo erectus. *These tools came from Bed IV at the famous Olduvai Gorge in Tanzania, scene of many important discoveries in the search for our origins. The carefully shaped handaxes, cleavers, and other items were found in rocks dating back 700,000 years.*

FROM EARLY HUMANS TO MAMMALS

The geological time scale starts with the formation of the Earth, some 4.6 billion years ago. The first and longest span of time was the Precambrian, where forms of life were mainly small, simple, and soft-bodied. The onset of the Cambrian about 570 million years ago marked the rise of shelled animals in the sea. There followed the "Ages" of Fish, Amphibians, and Reptiles, culminating in the domination of land by the dinosaurs, from about 200 to 65 million years ago.

Mammals first appeared more than 200 million years ago, but were overshadowed by the reptiles. But some 65 million years ago all the dinosaurs – as well as other groups of reptiles on land, in the sea and in the air, and certain other animal groups, and many plants too – became extinct over a relatively short period. (This was only one of several "mass extinctions" that have occurred through geological time.) The extinction marked the beginning of the Tertiary period and also the Age of Mammals. The Tertiary is divided into epochs, and developments in the primate group can be traced from the fossils they left in the rocks formed during this time.

The first hominids (members of our own family, Hominidae), crop up in the fossil record less than four million years ago. Mammalian evolution covers only about four percent of the Earth's entire history, and humans have been around for only 0.1 percent of the history of our planet.

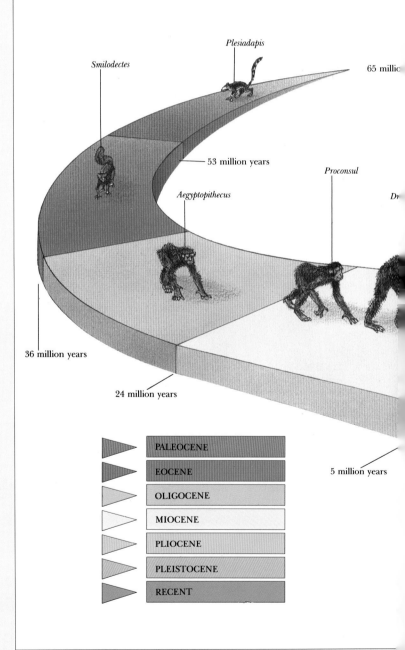

This scheme shows the epochs of the Tertiary period, the "Age of Mammals," and representative primates along the way. The earlier epochs were times of evolutionary experimentation, when bizarre and varied new forms of mammals appeared in a relatively short time. The placental mammals diversified from three or four groups that survived after the dinosaur extinction, to well over 40 groups by 50 million years ago.

All the living orders of placental mammals – from whales and bats to rodents and primates – came on the scene during those crucial years.

Primates can be traced through the succeeding epochs, as various monkeys and apes came and went. In more recent times, the dearth of fossil evidence for apes towards the end of the Miocene, which might indicate links between apes and hominids, is known as the "late Miocene gap."

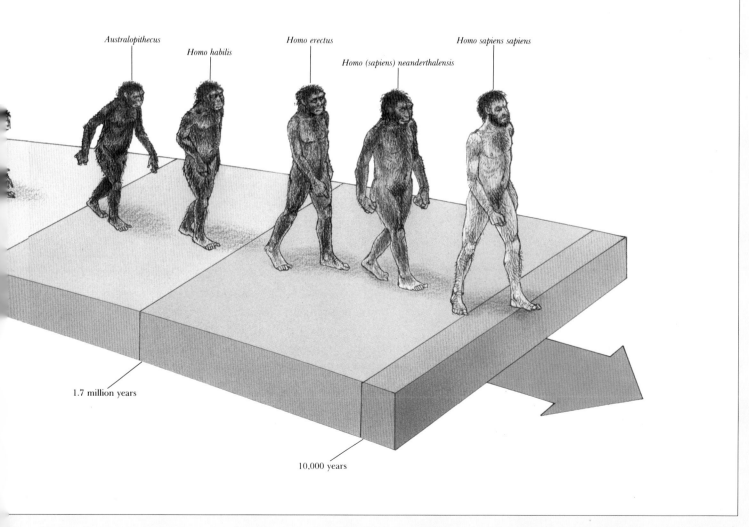

Australopithecus

Homo habilis

Homo erectus

Homo (sapiens) neanderthalensis

Homo sapiens sapiens

1.7 million years

10,000 years

CHAPTER

Defining The Human Species

Most of us are interested in our family history. Who was grandfather, and what was his job? Has our family lived in the area for a long time, or did we come from far away? Extend this natural curiosity, in both space and time. Where did the various groups of people around the world come from? How long have they lived in different regions, such as Australia or the Americas? Who were the first settlers in these places – and where did they come from? And going back still further, how, when, and where did human beings appear on the Earth? Who were our immediate, and our ultimate, ancestors?

The answers to these questions may help to explain why we are the way we are, and where we could be heading in the future. These are exciting times for the study of human evolution. Spectacular fossil discoveries during the past few decades are combining with tremendous advances in dating techniques, genetic analysis, linguistics, and several other scientific disciplines, to produce a startling new and widely discussed picture of the origins of Mankind.

Before we look into the past, we should clarify our terms. What, exactly, is a human? We need to define ourselves, by noting the similarities that make us a single group, and the differences that distinguish us from other living things. To do this, we must first understand how biologists view the living world.

CLASSIFICATION AND TAXONOMY

One of Linnaeus' great advances was his system of binomial nomenclature – two names for each natural group, or species, of plants and animals. This contrasted with other, clumsier systems of the time, which had six and even ten names for each kind. The first name is the generic or "family" name, given to a small group (the genus), within which the different members had obvious and close similarities. For example, the generic name for humans is *Homo*. The second name is for the basic taxonomic unit, the species. The original Linnean system has been modified and extended to cover more than a million known kinds of animals, and over 350,000 types of plants, as well as bacteria and other microscopic organisms. The hierarchy runs upwards from species to genus, family, order, class, phylum, and kingdom. Inbetween groups such as sub-phylum, supra-order, or tribe are incorporated as required.

FROM MAMMAL TO PRIMATE

Humans are obviously members of the kingdom *Animalia*. We move around, breathe, feed, breed, and do all the things a typical animal does. Moreover, along with fishes, amphibians, reptiles, and birds (as recognised by Aristotle), we belong in the phylum *Chordata*,

Use of fire is a behavioural feature unique to humans. Anatomically, the modern human being Homo sapiens *belongs to the apes-and-human group, Hominoidea. We are unusual among the living members of this group in having a large brain relative to body size, and an upright stance which involves walking habitually on two feet (bipedality). But there is a* whole galaxy of behavioural traits related to our "intelligence," from making tools to manipulating fire, which sets us apart from close relatives such as the chimpanzee, gorilla, and orangutan.

The typical primate's upright posture, when sitting on a bough or clinging to a tree trunk, converts to an all-fours position on the ground, as demonstrated by this macaque monkey in Kathmandu, Nepal.

In northwestern Europe the herring gull Larus argentatus *(below) shares its range with the lesser black-backed gull* Larus fuscus. *The two rarely interbreed – but they could! Towards eastern Europe and Asia, the herring gull disappears and the lesser black-backed gull becomes more like a herring gull in appearance. Towards the west, in North America, the reverse happens. This demonstrates that defining a species in nature is not always a clear-cut matter.*

subphylum *Vertebrata*. The important feature here is the backbone or vertebral column, one of the most crucial and significant evolutionary developments in the animal kingdom.

The next level is the class. Humans are placed in the class *Mammalia*, a group characterised by a constant body temperature (homeothermy or "warm-bloodedness"), possession of fur or hair, and milk-producing mammary glands for feeding the young. There are some 4,000 species of mammals, ranging from tiny shrews to huge elephants and giant whales.

Within the mammals, we are best placed in the order Primates, along with about 180 species of lemurs, lorises, tarsiers, monkeys, and apes. No single feature delineates the order, but in general, primates are mammals with relatively large brains, forward-facing eyes which give binocular or stereoscopic "3-D" vision (allowing them to judge distance and depth), well-developed colour discrimination, hands with opposable thumbs able to grip, and flat fingernails and toenails (rather than claws or hooves) which enhance the sensitivity of the finger- and toe-tips. Many modern primates habitually hold their bodies upright. The primate skeleton reflects this. It has two collar-bones or clavicles, which help to support and brace the arms and widen the range of shoulder movements – a useful feature for an animal that can carry its weight by its arms.

There are six fairly clear-cut groups of primates: lemurs, lorises, tarsiers, New World monkeys, Old World monkeys, and apes. The first three are sometimes referred to as prosimians; the last three are known as simians or as their own sub-order, *Anthropoidea*.

Anatomically we have most in common with the last-named group, the apes. These comprise the gorillas, chimpanzees, orangutans, and gibbons. Apes lack tails and have arms which are longer than their legs, and a specialised wrist structure that gives flexibility with strength. The trunk is not flattened from side to side, as in monkeys, but is more barrel-shaped. There are other

anatomical similarities among the apes, such as large body size and comparatively large brain, relatively flat face, and a continuous bowl-shaped bony structure, the eye socket, that encloses each eye within the skull and separates it from the jaw and face muscles. (This last feature is shared by the monkeys.)

The apparent lack of body hair on the human is not usually regarded as significant by biologists. In fact, we have just as many or even more hairs than gorillas and chimps. Over most of the human body, the hairs are simply very small.

The next group in the taxonomic hierarchy is the family. The consensus is that the smaller gibbons (nine species) of south-eastern Asia belong in one family, the *Hylobatidae* or "lesser apes." The larger orangutans (one species) from the same region, and the gorillas (one species) and chimps (two species, common and pygmy) from Africa, make up the family *Pongidae*, or "great apes." Humans are sufficiently distinct, anatomically, to form a third family: *Hominidae* (one living species).

THE SPECIES CONCEPT

This classification of the human species is carried out solely on anatomy, or body structure. A living species has many other characteristics that could also be incorporated into a classification, such as geographical distribution, behaviour, physiology (the way the body works down to the biochemical level), and choice of habitat. For instance, the apes live in open woodland or forested areas and (apart from the heaviest male gorillas) spend much time in trees. Thus anatomy is not the only guide. Indeed, the main plank in the biological definition of a "species" does not rely on anatomy, but on reproductive ability.

Members of a species can breed together to produce offspring, which are also able to breed successfully. Members from different species cannot do this. Even if individuals from two separate species are able to mate and give birth, the offspring are usually sterile and unable to reproduce more of their kind. For example, a male horse (species *Equus caballus*) can mate successfully with a female ass or donkey (species *Equus africanus or arsinus*), who gives birth to a hinny. A male ass and a female horse may likewise crossbreed, to produce a mule. But mules and hinnies are sterile. They are therefore both the beginnings and ends of their lines, and not new species.

THE VALIDITY OF OTHER GROUPINGS

This definition of a species holds reasonably well across the plant and animal kingdoms, from daisies to rhinos. In some cases it needs the help of other groupings near the species level, including sub-species, varieties, races, circular species, and clines (gradations). But in general it reflects the status of the species as relatively easy to recognise, and a natural biological grouping. Genera, families, and the other groups are artificial, being imposed as part of the taxonomic (classification) process. Different taxonomists may come to different conclusions as they select and study the similarities and differences between species, and so they may devise different classifications. Indeed; this happens quite often, especially among the lesser-known groups, and the subject is in a continuing state of flux.

BEHAVIOUR AND SOCIETY

Many animals live alone, coming together briefly to mate. Others may pair up only to rear offspring, or pair for life. In several groups, animals live communally and interact socially. The apes show complex behaviour in this area. It indicates their ability to show novel and inventive behaviour patterns, and to learn from one another. The apes also have in common an extended period of parental care for the young, compared to other mammals, which is known in biology as, K selection. Humans share these characteristics.

Gibbons These lesser apes live in pairs, usually for life. The male and female breed every second or third year and are accompanied by offspring of various ages, who, when they become mature, leave their parents" home range. The average gibbon group is a family of two parents and two or three young.

Orangs Orangutan males tend to be solitary, while the young stay with their mother. Occasionally adult females may band together, or young orangs may form their own small troops.

Gorillas The typical gorilla social group is based on the harem system. An older, dominant male leads the troop of about a dozen members. There are also a few young adult males, several adult females, and their offspring. These members stay together for many years, youngsters leaving for other groups when they become mature.

(Above) An Eastern lowland gorilla. The gorilla is the biggest of the ape species, and its populations are critically threatened - by its close relative Homo sapiens.

Chimps Chimpanzees have more complex societies still, with a greater range of social behaviours. The main unit is the community, of some 40-80 individuals. This is usually split into parties of 5-10 which forage for food, rest, groom each other, and play with the young. Sometimes they form hunting parties to capture and kill prey such as small monkeys. At other times males band together and aggressively patrol the borders of their community ranges. They will attack a lone male or a smaller party from the neighbouring community, occasionally inflicting fatal wounds. Continuing research reveals more fascinating intricacies of chimpanzee social behaviour.

Such varied and adaptable behaviour among the apes is partly due to their relatively large brains, and especially the large cerebrum, the "thinking" part of the brain. Medical research and evidence show that the human cerebrum is the dominant part of the brain for thought, sensations and body control, memory, and learning. This allows greater sophistication in control of the muscles for postures and gestures, especially of the face and hands. This is important in communication, speech, and tool-making. On an index comparing "cranial capacity" (the space inside the braincase, which is an indicator of brain size) with body weight, lemurs and lorises are in the range 3-6, monkeys around 4-8, apes 5-9, and humans 23.

UNIQUELY HUMAN?

Over the years, many features have been proposed as being unique to humans, marking us off from the other apes and primates, and accounting for our astounding success. On simple biological criteria, we are truly successful: the most numerous large creature on Earth, still increasing our species population at a phenomenal rate, having spread worldwide; able to survive successfully in every habitat, and with an unequalled power to alter the environment.

Evidence shows that some of these "uniquely human"

(Right) Various kinds of animals show co-operative group behaviour. Here African wild dogs work together to bring down a young wildebeest (gnu). The standard pattern of attack is for one dog (usually a dominant pack member) to grasp the victim's nose, with perhaps another hanging onto its tail, while the pack members disembowel it from the rear. Faced with such cooperation, few animals escape. Recent research has shown that chimps have a remarkable degree of organization and co-operation when they embark on "hunting parties."

characteristics occur in at least a few other species. The significance is not in their presence or absence, but in their degree of development, and the fact that they all occur together in *Homo sapiens*. (Most of these features are covered in detail in later chapters.)

THE BRIGHTEST APE

Foremost of human features is "intelligence": our abilities to think and understand, memorise, assess and solve problems, learn from the past and plan for the future, adapt and invent, and control and manipulate our surroundings, are unparalleled. Such brain-power underlies much of what we perceive as "human" behaviour and achievements. This includes communication and speech, tool-making and using, control of fire, cultural and ceremonial traits, and our social interactions.

Learning and problem-solving in a rudimentary form occur among several animals. Squirrels and blue tits can extract nuts from complex feeders, negotiating levers and mazes and other devices on the way. However, this type of behaviour is achieved chiefly by trial and error, testing various methods until one succeeds, and then repeating it thereafter. Only a few animals, such as chimps, seem able to think in more abstract terms and solve a problem mentally, rather than making numerous physical attempts. A chimp presented with food on a high shelf, and two or three wooden boxes, may pile up the boxes to make a tower, from which it can reach the food.

THE TALKATIVE APE

Another human feature is spoken language. We have an

(Top) A tool-user in action: a chimpanzee reaches out with a stick to retrieve food floating just out of reach. Tool-using was once cited as an exclusively human activity, but many examples have been discovered in nature.

(Bottom)A song thrush uses a stone as an anvil as it smashes open the shell of a luckless banded snail. The Egyptian vulture will pick up stones and drop them on the eggs of other birds, to break open their shells and gain access to the meal within.

THE TOOL-USING APE

At one time, it was believed that humans were the only animals to use tools. (The definition of "tool" varies but, in general, it is an object manipulated not as an end in itself – like eating a piece of food – but as an intermediate to achieve some further aim.) Then naturalists observed thrushes smashing snail shells on stone "anvils" to get at the flesh inside; sea otters cracking abalone shells using a pebble as a hammer; Egyptian vultures dropping stones on other birds" eggs to crack them and release the contents; and numerous other examples of animals using tools.

So the notion was taken one step back: humans are the only creatures to *make* tools, possibly using other tools to do so. Then chimps were seen to take a twig and strip off the side twiglets, so that they could poke it into a termite nest, to extract and lick off the juicy termites. Although limited in scope, they were modifying an item to use it as a tool. Again, it is the degree to which humans make and use their vast array of tools and other devices, rather than a unique ability to do so.

Using fire may well be uniquely human. Predatory animals take advantage of creatures burned and roasted and tenderised by a natural fire. But our association with fire includes not only capitalising on it for warmth and cooking, but also controlling it, maintaining it to stop it going out, and creating it when it is absent.

THE UPRIGHT APE

Humans are the only apes, indeed one of the few mammals, to move about on two feet, with the body upright. As mentioned previously, numerous primates have an upright posture as they cling to a tree trunk or sit on a branch. Humans have this too, but are unique in bipedality (walking on two legs), with arms swinging free. Walking is a form of "controlled falling" that helps to conserve energy, and allows dogged pursuit of prey, as well as carrying things while on the move.

It also has implications for the fine control of posture and balance, and for releasing the hands from moving duties, allowing them to be utilised in other ways. Along with the primate grasping and manipulating abilities, delicate sensations in the fingertips, and good stereoscopic vision to judge distance, freeing the hands may have been critical in the development of tool-making.

amazingly extensive repertoire of words and sounds. Speech is primarily a brain function, as we select the audible symbols we call words, and work out the syntax, tense, and sense of a sentence that will put our meaning across. The human larynx is well-developed compared to other primates, with its muscles finely controlled by a part of the brain set aside specifically for the purpose.

Of course, many animals communicate. Some do it visually, by signs and signals. This is obviously useful in open habitats where they can easily see their fellows, but less so in forests where the foliage obscures the view. Many animals also make sounds and communicate by vocalisations, which is a more effective long-distance method among the trees. Some, especially the monkeys and apes, have sophisticated whoops, gobbles, screeches, screams, and roars. However, none approaches our own linguistic achievements (page 133).

continued on page 24

DATING TECHNIQUES

For decades palaeontologists dreamed of being able to read the age of rocks and fossils. Today there are more than a dozen techniques for doing this. However, each has its limitations.

Relative dating, in its simplest form, means being able to tell whether one specimen is older or younger than another. Geologists and palaeontologists have devised a series of time periods spanning the history of the Earth (see pages 14-15), each characterised by formation of certain types of rocks. Some rocks and fossils can also be given *absolute* dates – the number of years before the present when they formed. Some absolute methods are based on radioactivity. As a rock forms, chemical substances are encapsulated within it. Some of these naturally give off radioactivity and change with time, turning from one form (or isotope) of an element into another, or even into a different element. This is called radioactive decay; the original substance is the "parent," and the new one is the "daughter." The decay occurs at a regular and characteristic rate for each parent substance. It is like a ticking clock, keeping time by its own destruction. It is usually measured by half-life: the time taken for half of the number of parent atoms, in a given sample, to decay into daughters. Working back from the relative amounts of parent and daughter, it is possible to calculate how long they have been encapsulated together – and so when the rock formed. The half-life of a substance limits its span of application. Also only some rocks can be radiodated, such as solidified lavas. Fossils may have to be dated by implication from the ages of the rock strata above or below them.

STRATIGRAPHY

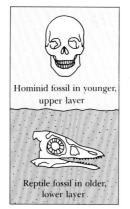

Hominid fossil in younger, upper layer

Reptile fossil in older, lower layer

Stratigraphy is the branch of geology concerned with the identification, naming and dating of stratified rocks – that is, rocks existing in strata (beds or layers), which may contain fossils. The law of superposition states that younger sedimentary rocks form on top of older ones. So fossils in sedimentary rocks nearer the surface represent animals and plants that lived more recently than those represented by fossils in deeper layers. But earthquakes, fault lines, mountain-building and volcanic eruptions split rock strata, bend them, tilt and even overturn them. In tipped-over layers, the rocks and fossils nearer the surface are older, not younger. Nevertheless, paleontologists have charted the fossils typical of each layer, especially abundant and rapidly changing microfossils such as pollen grains on land and tiny foraminiferans in the sea. This immense work has produced biostratigraphical (fossil) sequences which allow newly discovered fossils to be dated relatively, according to other fossils found with them, or the type of rock in which they are embedded.

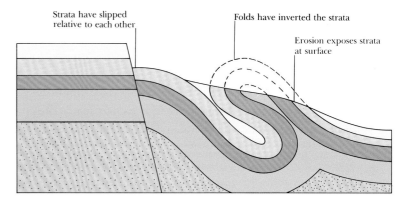

Strata have slipped relative to each other

Folds have inverted the strata

Erosion exposes strata at surface

FLUORINE-DATING

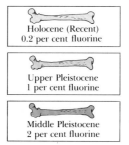

Holocene (Recent) 0.2 per cent fluorine

Upper Pleistocene 1 per cent fluorine

Middle Pleistocene 2 per cent fluorine

As a bone or tooth lies in the ground, turning into a fossil, it is subjected to great chemical change. In some areas, this involves absorbing the naturally present chemical fluorine from the ground water around it. Rates of fluorine absorption vary greatly, depending on its levels in the ground water. But fossils from different levels of the same site, or from comparable sites, can be dated relative to each other by analyzing their fluorine content. The more fluorine they hold (up to a "ceiling" saturation level), the longer they have been there. This method helped to expose the Piltdown fraud (page 36) and it has been a useful relative dating technique in certain areas.

RADIOMETRIC DATING

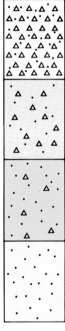

Time of excavation

A certain proportion of C-14 has decayed to the common form C-12

Time of formation

△ Carbon-12
· Carbon-14

Absolute dating by radioactive decay uses a series of decay sequences such as potassium-argon, rubidium-strontium, uranium-thorium-lead, and "carbon dating". The latter relies on measuring the residual levels of radioactive carbon-14 in the specimen. It is most useful for animal and plant remains up to 70,000–50,000 years old. A related technique, fission track dating, traces submicroscopic pathways that decaying uranium-238 particles make in a crystal.

PALEOMAGNETISM

Through the ages the Earth's magnetic North and South poles have wandered, changed in strength, and even reversed. Paleomagnetism is the study of the history of the Earth's magnetic field, as revealed by evidence from rocks. As igneous rocks form from cooling molten lava or magma, any tiny particles or magnetite (a naturally magnetic mineral) they contain line up according to the Earth's magnetic field at the time. Modern scientific instruments measure the direction and degree of particle alignment, allowing the geologist to produce a magnetic chronology. Fossils can be dated from igneous rocks above or below them.

A number of major disruptions to the Earth's magnetic field – events – have been identified and named. Longer periods of magnetic stability are known as epochs.

Normal magnetic field, magnetic North Pole at geographical North Pole

Reversed magnetic field, magnetic North Pole at geographical South Pole

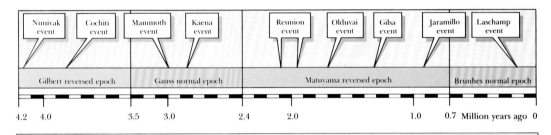

ELECTRON-SPIN RESONANCE (ESR)

In each atom of a substance, electrons orbit the central nucleus. The electrons have a certain amount of resonance or "vibration" according to features such as the time since that substance became stabilized. ESR measures this resonance under the effect of a powerful magnetic field, by absorption of microwaves or other waves beamed through the specimen. (A similar method called NMR, nuclear magnetic resonance, is one form of medical "scan" that can give an image of organs within the body.)

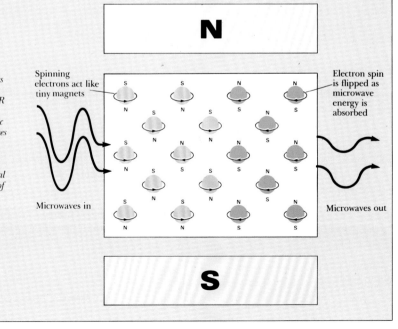

MOLECULAR COMPARISONS

In the last few decades, molecular biologists have been comparing equivalent molecules from the bodies of different animals, in the same way that anatomists compare the shapes of bones or muscles. These studies have corroborated much of the taxonomy based on gross anatomy and other characteristics.

One of the star performers in this field is the protein myoglobin, a main constituent of muscle tissue. In mammals, each molecule of myoglobin is made of 153 subunits called amino acids, joined like beads on a string. Muscle tissue samples are treated with enzymes and other chemicals to isolate the myoglobin, which is then snipped into shorter lengths of amino acid chains by more specialised enzymes. Analysis of the different lengths by techniques such as chromatography and electrophoresis gives a "linear map," showing the identity and order of the amino acids along the myoglobin

chain. Human, gorilla, and chimp myoglobins differ by only one amino acid each. Gibbons differ by another amino acid; baboons by another five; and other Old World monkeys and then New World monkeys by increasing numbers of amino acids.

Many other molecules have been similarly studied, including haemoglobins which carry oxygen in the blood, fibrinopeptides involved in blood clotting, immunological proteins from the body's immune defence system, and alpha-crystallin A protein in the lens of the eye. The results mostly confirm the accepted classifications. Humans, chimps, and gorillas have a very similar "molecular anatomy."

GENETIC AND CHROMOSOMAL COMPARISONS

The molecules mentioned above are produced from a "blueprint" carried in the animal's genes. It is possible

THE HUMAN SKULL

Skulls and teeth feature heavily in the search for our origins. Teeth, in particular, fossilise well. The shapes and curvatures of the 22 bones which make up the main skull provide much information, such as the size of the cavity which houses the brain. This "braincase" is formed

from eight curved, firmly-joined bones, sometimes called the cranium or calvaria. There are 14 bones in the facial area. The term cranium is also used to refer to the whole structure, excluding the mandible.

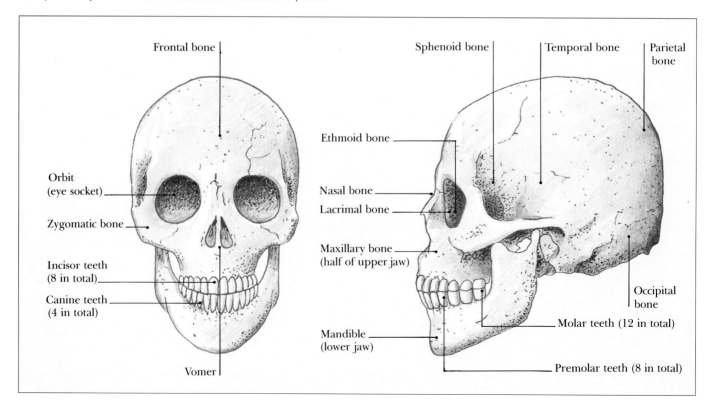

Frontal bone

Sphenoid bone

Temporal bone

Parietal bone

Ethmoid bone

Orbit (eye socket)

Nasal bone

Lacrimal bone

Zygomatic bone

Maxillary bone (half of upper jaw)

Incisor teeth (8 in total)

Canine teeth (4 in total)

Occipital bone

Molar teeth (12 in total)

Mandible (lower jaw)

Premolar teeth (8 in total)

Vomer

to compare these genes directly by studying the chemical which comprises them – deoxyribonucleic acid, or DNA. This is an immensely long molecular string made up of four types of sub-units called bases, arranged in coded sequences. The DNA from different animals can be isolated and its base sequences determined and compared (this is explained in more detail in Chapter Seven).

In a body cell, DNA is tightly coiled and wrapped into larger packages, the chromosomes, which can be seen under a powerful microscope. The numbers, size, shape, and the detailed striped patterns (banding pattern) of the chromosomes are further criteria which can be compared and contrasted between species. There is also DNA in the tiny bodies within each cell known as mitochondria (mt-DNA, page 128).

These studies again confirm the taxonomic groupings based on anatomy. They place the human species among the ape families, and emphasise the similarity between humans and the other great apes.

So we know where we are now. With a slight shift in viewpoint, all of these studies can give us an angle into the past, to begin the study of where we came from.

TAXONOMY AND EVOLUTION

Charles Darwin's theory of evolution brought several new perspectives to the Linnean taxonomic groupings: suddenly they became evolutionary groups, too. Animals which were very similar to each other were closely related. They had inherited many of their characteristics from a common ancestor. This applied at each level of the taxonomic hierarchy, from minor differences between individuals of a species, to broader and more significant similarities up through the genus and family levels, to order, phylum, and kingdom. Assuming a particular feature was inherited, it was possible to trace it through the groups and propose where it first arose, and how it was then modified.

Another great advance was to regard an animal's characteristics as *adaptive*, rather than existing in a vacuum, subject to the fancies of a creator. Evolutionary theory showed that each feature of the body was shaped by natural selection in some way, so that it contributed to the animal's survival, by adapting it better to the prevailing conditions.

A third advance was the realisation that it was now possible to make sense of fossils.

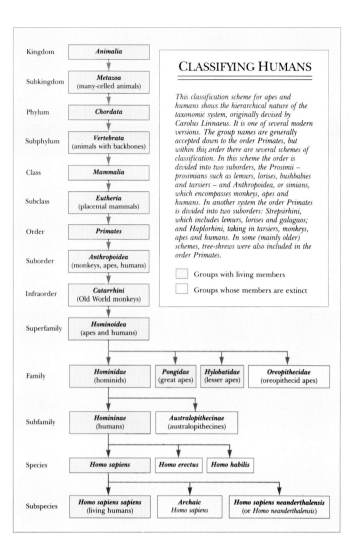

CLASSIFYING HUMANS

This classification scheme for apes and humans shows the hierarchical nature of the taxonomic system, originally devised by Carolus Linnaeus. It is one of several modern versions. The group names are generally accepted down to the order Primates, but within this order there are several schemes of classification. In this scheme the order is divided into two suborders, the Prosimii – prosimians such as lemurs, lorises, bushbabies and tarsiers – and Anthropoidea, or simians, which encompasses monkeys, apes and humans. In another system the order Primates is divided into two suborders: Strepsirhini, which includes lemurs, lorises and galagaos; and Haplorhini, taking in tarsiers, monkeys, apes and humans. In some (mainly older) schemes, tree-shrews were also included in the order Primates.

☐ Groups with living members

☐ Groups whose members are extinct

SNAPSHOTS OF THE PAST

Fossils are the remains of long-dead plants and animals, preserved in the rocks. Mostly they are formed from hard parts such as bones, teeth, shells, bark, seeds, and leaf veins. In exceptional cases, soft parts are preserved, such as skin and hair; even whole insects, fish, crustaceans, and leaves have been found imprisoned in rock.

Fossils are almost invariably found in sedimentary rocks. These began as layers of particles called sediments which were laid down by water in a river, lake or sea, or as blankets of windblown sand in a desert. As the rock forms, the remains of animals and plants trapped in the sediments become changed chemically, and turn to stone, or fossils. A fossil is therefore a "snapshot of the past," a piece of animal or plant that gives a glimpse into life in former times. The study of animal fossils is known as palaeontology.

HOW FOSSILS FORM

Fossilisation occurs in a fairly predictable sequence of events, but at each stage, both specimens and information are lost.
As the carcass decomposes, soft tissues generally soon disappear to scavengers and bacteria (1). The hard parts – usually teeth and bones – may be left undamaged, but they could eventually disintegrate if left exposed to the air. A fortuitous shower of lava ash from a nearby volcano may cover the bones to prevent this (2).
As further layers build up, the buried parts undergo changes (3).

The spaces in the bone may become permineralised, as minerals in water solution in the rock infiltrate and solidify. Or the bony tissue itself is replaced crystal by crystal, by another hard mineral. Slowly, the remains are petrified or "turned to stone." Over the course of geological time, the rocks may be uplifted or tilted, and erosion exposes the ancient sediments and the fossilised bones they contain (4).

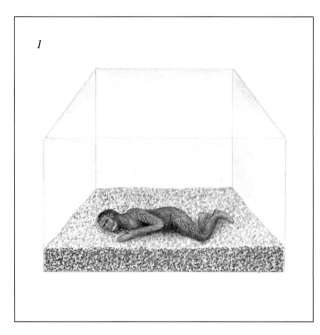

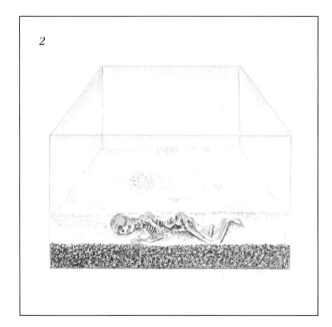

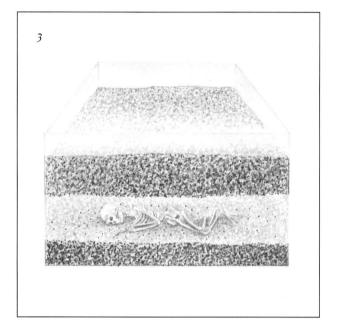

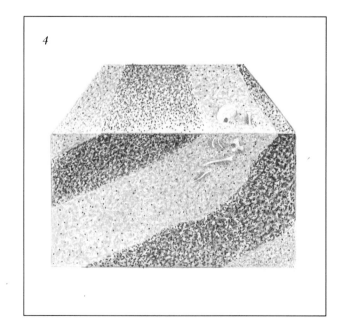

The standard "evolutionary trees" show how various groups changed, died out, merged, or split through time. The older versions combined fossil evidence with comparative anatomy. Modern versions also take evidence from physiology, ecology and behaviour, and chromosomal, genetic, and molecular analysis. With all these means at our disposal, it is appropriate to jump back in time millions of years, in order to search for our origins.

PROBLEMS WITH PREHISTORIC SPECIES

The evidence from comparative studies of present-day species can be combined with the evidence of fossils submitted to techniques such as cladistic analysis. The aim is to postulate some kind of "evolutionary tree" for ourselves, our ancestors, and our close relatives. But there are problems, theoretical and practical. A living species is defined by reproductive criteria. Its members can breed together, but are unable to make fertile matings with members of other species. Fossils cannot breed. They are lumps of stone. As for the creatures they represent, we can make educated guesses at reconstructions of their bodies, but we have no direct way of knowing about their breeding habits.

It is assumed that because species exist today, they existed in the past. However, it is not possible to use reproductive criteria to describe a past species, or *palaeospecies* (one known only from fossils). The morphology (shape and form) of the fossil, and the physiology it implies, must suffice. This means people, usually palaeontologists, draw the lines between species. It makes the definition of a palaeospecies a more subjective process.

One type of line can be drawn between groups of animals which were alive at the same time in the past, and which their fossils show to be very similar. Do the fossils represent one species whose members were diverse, or do they represent more than one species, as with the australopithecines (page 64). Another type of line is drawn in time. Evolution may bring about a change in a group of animals, and eventually the species becomes quite different. At which point did the old species end and the new one begin? This is relevant to the emergence of our present human species from its possible ancestor, *Homo erectus* (Chapter Five).

Another difficulty is that fossilisation is a rare and fairly random event. The chances of a dead animal (or plant) not being crunched up by scavengers or decom-

Modern African apes, the gorilla (above) and the two species of chimpanzees, live in habitats where they are unlikely to be preserved as fossils. It is more probable that their bones will be scavenged and destroyed or will decay in the jungles and savanna woodlands, rather than be covered with sediments in water or with windblown sand. In fact there is no fossil record to speak of for the living African great ape species.

posed, but rather coming to rest in a place where it is likely to fossilise; and then the fossils remaining intact over the millennia, without being distorted beyond recognition or sinking into the Earth's crust and melting; and then the fossils eventually being exposed on the surface; and then the fossils being recognised for what they are by a fossil-hunter, and being excavated and studied ... become more remote at each stage. Therefore our reconstructions of the past are biased by the great gaps and extreme patchiness in the fossil record.

The evolution of new species is generally a population phenomenon. It occurs over time among groups, or populations, of animals. Fossils represent a very tiny and random sample of the creatures that were in existence at a given time.

CLADES AND CLADOGRAMS

Enormous amounts of information are being obtained from fossils, genes, and comparative studies of anatomy and physiology. The data is important – and so are the methods of analysing it.

Cladistics is a powerful analytical method developed in the 1970s. It involves the search for clades. A clade is

continued on page 28

a group that includes all the descendants of a single ancestor. It is a monophyletic or 'single-origin" group. Such groups are marked by the sharing of at least one unique feature – a characteristic that the common ancestor developed (through evolution), and passed on to all of its descendants.

A familiar example of a clade is the birds. Their unique feature is the feather. All birds have feathers, and no other animals have them. Feathers are complex structures and are assumed to have evolved just once, in the ancestral birds. They have since been passed on to all their descendants. Such a unique characteristic, derived from the common ancestor, and shared by members of the clade, is known as a *synapomorphy*.

However, the characteristic must be carefully selected. All birds have backbones, yet possessing a backbone would not be sufficient to define birds as a clade. Mammals, reptiles, amphibians, and fish also have backbones. This scrutiny is known as submitting the chosen characteristic to an "out-group comparison" –

examining other groups to see if they possess it, too.

When carrying out cladistic analysis, the boundaries of study are drawn in a broad way, and an intensive search for suitable characteristics is made among all the species of the group in question. The search can include fossils, too, if they are compared with the same parts of living species. The characteristics are tested by out-group comparisons to find the synapomorphies.

The species are then arranged in a treelike branching diagram called a cladogram. Each branching point is a two-way or dichotomous split. It is called a node, and it is defined by one (or more) synapomorphies. All of the species in the smaller clades share this unique feature. The species in the larger clades do not necessarily have it. Thus each node defines a clade. The clades "nest" neatly, two smaller ones within each larger one, and so on along the hierarchy.

One problem with cladograms is finding the "right" synapomorphies. This is especially acute when dealing with fossils and the fossil record is scarce and fragmentary, as it is for primates, apes, and hominids.

EVOLUTIONARY TREES AND THE ENVIRONMENT

Cladistics is basically a sorting technique that indicates relationships only. All of its species, living and extinct, are placed in a line on the diagram. A cladogram has no timescale.

Most people are more familiar with the "evolutionary tree," also known as a phylogenetic tree or phylogeny. This has a timescale. The various groups are placed in correct chronological order, according to the dating of their fossil record. Their relationships are shown by a variety of branching conventions. In the search for our origins, the aim is to construct a phylogeny for living and extinct humans, their ancestors and their close relatives, which is as consistent and complete as possible with the various strands of evidence. Cladistics gives a theoretical construct, but it is only one step in this overall aim.

Constructing an evolutionary tree is not done solely in the laboratory and on the computer. It is necessary to look at nature itself, to see why animals and plants evolve as they do. Environmental change is the powerful force that directs evolution. The environments of today are readily observable. It is possible to gain some idea of environments in the past, and the types of habi-

Olive baboons forage for food. In evolutionary biology, it is said that "in Africa, the history of baboon species is the history of the grasslands." In times past, open woodland and savanna spread at the expense of thick forest, due to factors such as a drier climate. The baboons took advantage of this spreading habitat and forsook the usual primate tree-dwelling. They walk and run easily on all fours, and are the most herbivorous and ground-living of all Old World monkeys.

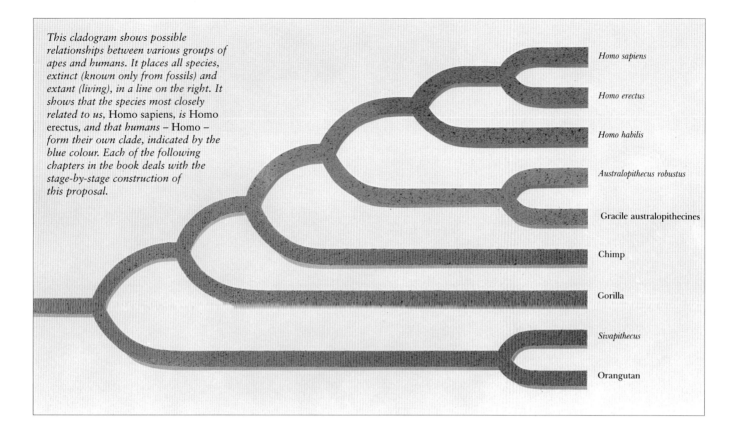

This cladogram shows possible relationships between various groups of apes and humans. It places all species, extinct (known only from fossils) and extant (living), in a line on the right. It shows that the species most closely related to us, Homo sapiens, is Homo erectus, and that humans – Homo – form their own clade, indicated by the blue colour. Each of the following chapters in the book deals with the stage-by-stage construction of this proposal.

Homo sapiens

Homo erectus

Homo habilis

Australopithecus robustus

Gracile australopithecines

Chimp

Gorilla

Sivapithecus

Orangutan

tats present, from the fossils that have been preserved. This study is the realm of palaeoecology.

For example, plant fossils from the Oligocene epoch, which lasted from about 38 to 26 million years ago, show that leafy trees and succulent plants were common in many regions. This indicates a moist climate at the time. The animals, particularly the mammals, resembled the forest browsers of today. Tree-dwelling primates were in their element.

During the next epoch, the Miocene (26 to 7 million years ago), plant fossils show that the forests shrank, especially in North America and Asia, to be replaced by savanna-type grassland habitats. Grasses are plants suited to a cooler, drier climate, and so the vegetation probably adapted to a changing climate. In turn, animal groups adapted to the changing vegetation. Large grazing herbivores developed, such as horses, camels, rhinos, and cattle. They had bigger, stronger teeth for chewing the tougher, less nutritious grasses.

The animal community had evolved in response to an environmental change. It may have been this same change that brought our distant ancestors down out of the trees, to take their first steps upon the ground.

CHAPTER

HUMAN ORIGINS

The quest for our ultimate origins begins with the origin of life itself. The Earth is about 4.6 billion years old. Fossil evidence shows that small, simple organisms were living at least 3 billion years ago.

A great deal of evidence supports the notion that all present-day organisms are related to each other, and that all of them – forms as diverse as slime moulds and elephants, oak trees and beetles, roses and humans – ultimately arose from a single common ancestor, some 3.5 billion years ago. This means that a single evolutionary tree, or phylogeny, relates all organisms, living and extinct.

Biologists and palaeontologists assume that life evolved from its simple beginnings through a succession of stages, as represented in the fossil record, toward the present-day diversity of some 10–30 million species. This does not mean that today's diversity is in some way the destiny or end-point of evolution; there has been great diversity in the past, and there may be in the future.

THE ORIGIN OF PRIMATES

Following the small-and-simple early life forms, larger animals with more complex bodies were living in the seas around 700 million years ago. The first vertebrates (animals with backbones) were early fish, that swam in the ancient seas about 500 million years ago. Some 100 million years later the first jawed creatures – also fish – appeared. The first land vertebrates were amphibians, walking along riverbanks around 380 million years ago. Reptiles were increasing their numbers and diversity by 300 million years ago. By 200 million years ago, as dinosaurs were beginning to dominate the land, the mammals had arrived.

The earliest mammal fossils are from the late Triassic period, 220–210 million years ago, from Europe. The animals themselves were shrew- or mouse-sized, and probably ate insects. For 150 million years during the "Age of Dinosaurs" the mammals continued to evolve, but they never became particularly numerous, and none was larger than a pet cat.

It is thought that the dominant present-day group of mammals, the placentals, appeared by the end of the Cretaceous period, 65 million years ago. Placentals differ from the two other mammal groups – the egg-laying monotremes (only two kinds remaining, the platypus and echidnas), and the marsupials (kangaroos, koalas, and opossums) – in that their young develop to a relatively advanced stage in the womb. The young are nourished from the mother's blood before birth by a specialised organ known as the placenta.

Around 64 million years ago, the dinosaurs and many other large reptiles mysteriously disappeared, along

30

A spider monkey clings with all five limbs (the fifth being its prehensile tail) to the boughs of a forest tree in tropical South America. Tree-dwelling has been a hallmark of the primate group – today represented by lemurs, tarsiers, bushbabies, monkeys and apes – for more than 50 million years. One of the great changes in the evolution of humans was a move toward ground-dwelling.

with some groups of sea creatures and plants. Mammals survived. In what could be pictured as the post-dinosaur "empty landscape," the mammals rapidly multiplied and diversified as they took advantage of the newly available food supplies and living places. By 55 million years ago, numerous groups had become established. One of these was the primates.

The earliest evidence of primates in the fossil record is sometimes cited as a single tooth, a molar from the lower jaw, dating from the late Cretaceous period about 67 million years ago. Dinosaurs roamed the area where it was found, which is now eastern Montana.

Teeth figure very prominently in the fossil record. Tooth enamel is the hardest and most durable substance in the body, and the part least likely to be scavenged or to decay after death. It is therefore the part most likely to fossilise. The sizes of the teeth, and their numbers and arrangement in the jaws (the dental formula), are very significant evolutionary pointers. A great bonus is that the general shapes and wear patterns of teeth are good clues to diet, and so to lifestyle and habitat (page 42).

Several features of this particular tooth place it in the primate group. A species has been named from it, *Purgatorius ceratops*, after Purgatory Hill, the site where it was discovered, and the dinosaur *Triceratops*, whose fossils were found in the same ancient brook bed.

Some experts reserve judgement on this slim evidence. Some also propose that the appearance of quite diverse primates by 55 million years ago means that the group had been evolving and diversifying for a long period before this, possibly back to 80–100 million years before the present. The fossils have not yet been found.

EARLY PRIMATES

A much better-known early primate is *Plesiadapis*, whose fossils date from the Paleocene epoch, about 57 million years ago. The fossils, of skulls and partial skeletons and especially teeth, show that there may have been several species of this genus living in North America and Europe.

During the Paleocene and succeeding Eocene epochs, to about 36 million years ago, fossils reveal that the primates underwent several bursts of evolution. The lemurs, tarsiers, and bushbabies appeared – tree-dwelling primates often referred to as prosimians, since they have less advanced features than the monkeys, apes, and humans, which are called simians.

Simian fossils first crop up in rocks from the Eocene period. They indicate monkey-like creatures, and two separate lines eventually become evident: the Old World monkeys of Europe, Africa, and Asia, and the New

PLESIADAPIS

Fleshed-out reconstructions of Plesiadapis *show a creature rather like a modern lemur, with clawed feet gripping the branches. This Paleocene tree-dweller has been traditionally classified as an early or archaic primate, mainly on the basis of its fossilised teeth. But recent discoveries of other skeletal parts have led to doubts about this interpretation.*

PRIMATE EVOLUTION

This is one version of the phylogenetic or evolutionary tree for extant groups of Primates. As with other mammals, primates went through several bursts of evolution during the Tertiary era, from about 65 million years ago. One of the earliest major splits was between the lemur-loris branch and the tarsiers and simians (monkeys, apes and, eventually, humans).

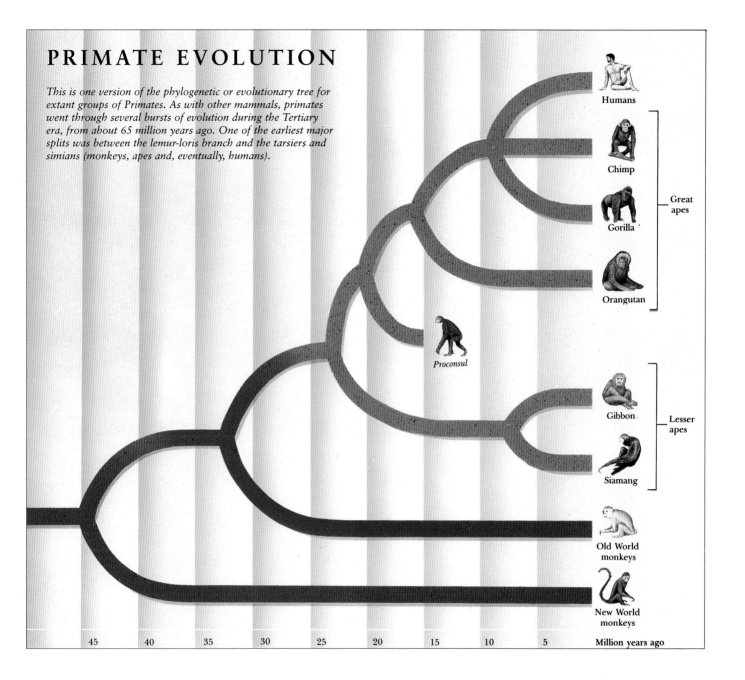

Humans

Chimp

Gorilla

Great apes

Orangutan

Proconsul

Gibbon

Lesser apes

Siamang

Old World monkeys

New World monkeys

| 45 | 40 | 35 | 30 | 25 | 20 | 15 | 10 | 5 | Million years ago |

World ones of the Americas. Today these two monkey groups look similar on the outside, but are quite distinct. New World monkeys (platyrrhines) generally have prehensile tails, splayed-apart nostrils and 36 teeth. Old World monkeys have close-set nostrils and 32 teeth, and lack prehensile tails. Studies of their body molecules reinforce this partition (page 22).

TOWARDS THE APES

One particularly rich fossil site is the Fayum depression region of Egypt. It is rocky, arid, "badland" country at the Saharan edge, where winds continually erode the surface rocks. These were once riverbed sediments; fossilised trees and woodland animals show that during the Oligocene epoch (36–24 million years ago), the area was covered with lush warm forests and rivers that flowed slowly north into the Mediterranean.

The Fayum fossils are dated at 35–30 million years old. With one questionable exception (the Eocene Azibius) they include the oldest primate remains in Africa. Of special interest is a monkeylike creature known as *Aegyptopithecus* ("ape from Egypt"). Since the 1960s, expeditions have recovered teeth and parts of

AEGYPTOPITHECUS

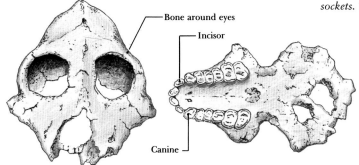

Bone around eyes

Incisor

Canine

One of the fossil faces of Aegyptopithecus (left), showing the bony growths around the eyes forming the eye orbits, or eye sockets. The underside view of the upper jaw, teeth, palate, and base of the skull (right) shows four incisor teeth at the front, a the prominent canines on either side.

The grasping foot of a modern-day concolor gibbon, Hylobates concolor, *from southeastern Asia (below). The very long and divergent big toe has evolved specifically to wrap around branches in the opposite direction to the other toes, producing a secure grip. This is a common adaptation in tree-dwellers. Note also the rough skin of the sole, which helps to increase purchase against the bark.*

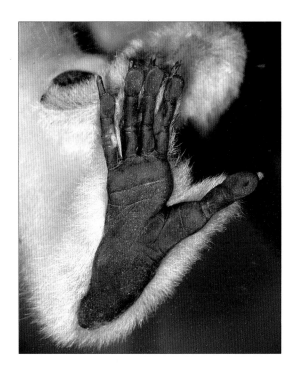

the skulls of four individuals. One fossilised skull is fairly complete, with the front part of the braincase the only major missing part. None of these skulls is associated with any "postcranial elements" – the palaeontologist's term for parts of the skeleton other than the skull, such as the spine and limb bones. However, individual bones and bone fragments from the rest of the skeleton are scattered in other places at the site, and judging by their size, shape, and numbers, probably came from *Aegyptopithecus* and a similar creature, *Apidium*.

Aegyptopithecus has been variously classified as a monkey, an ape, and neither (but still a primate). It has the reduced number of teeth and the bony eye sockets characteristic of simians, but no feature that would unambiguously place it in either the monkey or ape group. This may simply be because the monkey and ape groups, as we know them today, had not yet evolved. The first substantial fossils of Old World monkeys date only to 10 million years ago, with a few possible remains at 18 million years ago. The common view that simian ancestors evolved "through" the monkey stage into apes, and then into humans, may be incorrect. The first Old World monkeys may have evolved from what we would view as early apes.

One modern view is that *Aegyptopithecus* is related to early apes; while another primate from slightly older rocks at Fayum, *Parapithecus* (known from a sole piece of lower jaw), is related to the Old World monkeys, along with *Apidium*. It is tempting to draw many conclusions from the various primates preserved from Fayum, particularly since hardly any other fossil simians of this age have been found elsewhere. It has been pointed out, though, that despite these remains having yielded so much information, it is unlikely that the ancestral

forms of the major simian groups, perhaps together with their common ancestor, were all preserved together at the same small geographical site!

In life, *Aegyptopithecus* was about as big as a New World monkey such as the howler. (Another puzzling fact concerning the Fayum fossils is that, in general, they have several features in common with New World monkeys, despite being found in the Old World.) It was a tree-dweller, being able to grasp branches and climb with all four limbs. Males had long canine teeth which they may have used for specialised feeding, threat displays, or fighting off predators or rival males.

Modern simians live in groups. *Aegyptopithecus* probably did too. It ate tropical tree fruits and must have run into competition against the other animals represented in the Fayum fossils, including other primates, cat-like carnivores, hyraxes (small relatives of elephants), and various rodents.

MIOCENE APES

About 10 million years after *Aegyptopithecus* sat in the branches of North Africa, a similar-looking primate did the same in East Africa. This was *Dendropithecus*, the "wood ape." Although the Rift Valley of East Africa is now a mosaic of lowland grassy plains and forested mountains, 22 million years ago it was flatter and more evenly cloaked with tropical trees. This similarity of habitat is partly responsible for the similarity between *Aegyptopithecus* and *Dendropithecus*. Both were fruit-eating primates, though the latter was probably more active and mobile. However, *Dendropithecus* has several features which put it much closer to the hominoids (apes and humans), such as a rounder, flatter face (unlike the projecting "muzzle" of *Aegyptopithecus*), and more ape-like arm bones.

Another Miocene hominoid was *Heliopithecus*, the "sun ape," named because its fossils were first discovered in the glaring heat of the Arabian desert. It lived 17 million years ago in the forests that then covered the region. This creature is significant because its fossilised teeth show the trend toward a much thicker covering of enamel (as seen in many later apes and ourselves), compared to earlier primates. Extra wear-resistant enamel meant the teeth would last longer, and so their owner would be able to feed to a greater age. In animals such as elephants, when the teeth wear away, starvation ensues.

In a later hominoid, *Kenyapithecus* of 14 million years ago, the enamel is even thicker. This trend may have been guided by the changing environment. The woodlands of the time were probably less lush and fruitful, and without a year-round food supply. There may have been an annual dry season, when plant growth ceased. Teeth with thick enamel would have been an asset, allowing the hominoids to chew up tougher plant foods and so survive the dry season with a larger proportion of their enamel intact.

THE PUZZLES OF PROCONSUL

In 1927, a white settler in western Kenya was digging limestone from a quarry. He found some fossils embedded in the rock and sent them to the British Museum in London. When the rock was cleaned away, the fossils were recognised as part of the upper jawbone and tooth of a hominoid. Other fossils from the site gave an age of about 18 million years, fairly early in the Miocene epoch. Tindell Hopwood, who studied the fossils, realised that this was a startling find, partly because ape fossils were very rare, and especially because these remains were so old. He organised an expedition to the site in 1931 and collected two more fossils. Two years later, the world was presented with "the chimpanzee's ancestor" – *Proconsul africanus*.

This name has, for palaeontology, an unusually light-hearted derivation. In the 1930s a real chimp called Consul lived at London Zoo and performed tricks such as bicycle-riding and pipe-smoking. Hopwood's name referred to the imaginary predecessor of this entertainer, "Pro-Consul." (Some experts refer to Proconsul as

continued on page 38

PROCONSUL

A reconstruction of Proconsul africanus, *one of the species in the varied* Proconsul *genus from Miocene East Africa. Although it resembles a modern-day chimpanzee, all four of Proconsul's limbs were approximately the same length, whereas the chimp's arms are longer than its legs.*

PILTDOWN MAN

"Piltdown Man" was reconstructed from fossils dug out of a gravel bed at Piltdown Common in Sussex, southern England, in about 1912. The remains were discovered by amateur archeologist Charles Dawson, who with Arthur Smith Woodward, Keeper of Geology at London's Natural History Museum, searched the site. They turned up a total of nine pieces of cranium (braincase), mostly from the skull's left side; the right part of a lower jaw with two molar teeth; some flint tools; and the fossil bones of extinct animals. From these and other clues, the remains were dated at about 200,000 years old.

The pieced-together skull was certainly human, if rather primitive in certain features. But the ape-like lower jaw jutted out, and had a receding chin. If Charles Darwin's theory of evolution was correct, one might expect such an "evolutionary mosaic." "Piltdown Man" was therefore an ideal missing link, a composite of human and ape. He and his kind were named *Eoanthropus dawsoni*, "Dawn Man of Dawson."

Intense discussion continued. Were the skull and jaw part of the same individual, or did they just come to lie near each other by chance? During the next 30 years, ancient hominid fossils were discovered across Africa and Asia. However, none corroborated the evidence of *Eoanthropus*. Piltdown found itself further and further out on a limb. In 1948 the Piltdown specimens were subjected to the then newly developed technique of fluorine dating. The results caused a sensation. The fluorine contents of the skull and the jaw were far too low for the remains to be of any significant age. Further investigations revealed:

The jaw looked so ape-like because it was – it came from a medieval orangutan that died at about the age of 10.

The skull pieces were older than the jaw, but were not of significant age.

The isolated canine tooth was, like the lower jaw, relatively young. It had been filed down to look worn and coloured like the jaw.

For some 40 years, many expert scientists had been deceived. Who were the culprits? Investigators have since delved into the episode, but no definite proof has emerged. Why did the hoax succeed for so long? Piltdown fitted so well with what people hoped for at the time: an

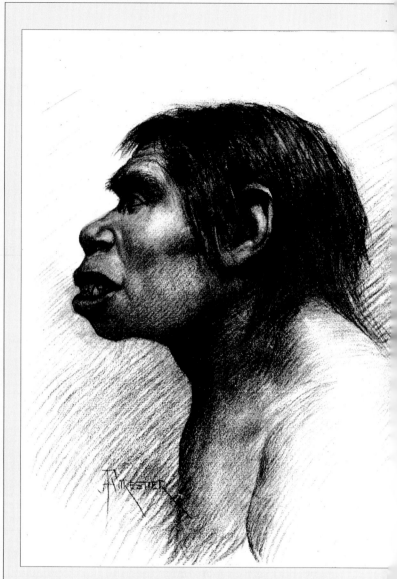

A reconstruction by artist A Forestier of the "Dawn Man" Eoanthropus, now commonly referred to as Piltdown Man, but known at the time of its discovery as Sussex Man. The London Illustrated News *pointed out that his "lower jaw is unmistakably ape-like, while presenting other features as indubitably human".*

evolutionary "missing link" combining features of human and ape. It demonstrated that what we expect to find may colour the interpretation of what we actually do find.

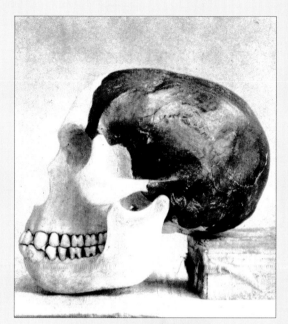

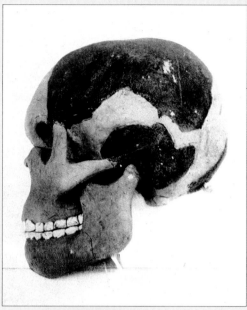

Smith Woodward's initial reconstruction of the Piltdown fossils (left) gave the skull's owner a jutting jaw, receding chin, and a relatively small brain volume of about 1,070 millilitres.

A rival Piltdown reconstruction (right) by Professor Arthur Keith, Conservator at the Museum of London's Royal College of Surgeons. The jaws jut less, and the brain volume is now 1,500 millilitres.

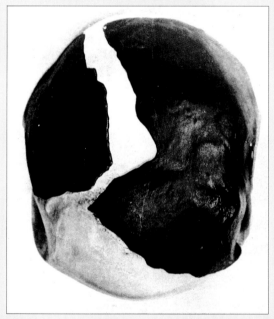

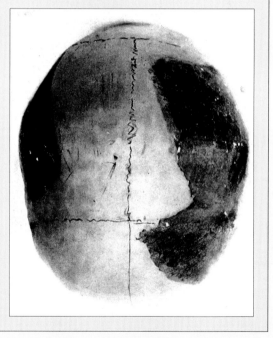

A view from above of Smith Woodward's version (left). It was criticized for its positioning of "the great blood channel", which Keith suggested was about one inch to the right of its correct position.

The top view of Keith's version (right) shows the actual fossils (dark pieces) more widely separated. This enlarged the space inside the braincase, producing "a really large brain for a modern man".

Dryopithecus, page 42.)

In 1948, Mary Leakey found fossils of the face and jaws of another *Proconsul* specimen on Rusinga Island, in Lake Victoria. In 1951 parts of a skull, arm and hand, and foot were discovered at the same site. In the 1980s, by a series of coincidences and palaeontological detective work, each of these finds was reunited with further fragments belonging to it. Pieces of the back of the 1948 skull had been found at the same place a year earlier, by Louis Leakey. He suspected they were from a primate, but lacking further discoveries, the pieces were consigned to a drawer of turtle fossils in Kenya's National Museum, in Nairobi. Some of the missing bones from the 1951 find were recognised in a collection of pig bones, at the same museum, and reunited to produce a more complete skeleton.

Recent excavations and reconstructions have produced many more *Proconsul* finds. At Kaswanga, also on Rusinga, parts of nine *Proconsul* skeletons were painstakingly recovered. They represent adults, youngsters, and babies. Now almost every bone in *Proconsul's* body is known.

LIFE IN THE EARLY MIOCENE

The current *Proconsul* evidence indicates that the picture is much more complicated than it appeared 20 years ago. It now seems that there were at least two and probably more species of this genus alive 18 million years ago. *Proconsul africanus* was small, weighing about 25 pounds in life, and had a brain volume of around 165 millilitres. *Proconsul nyanzae* was chimp-sized, and *Proconsul major* possibly as big as a gorilla. The early interpretations which emphasised *Proconsul's* acrobatic, leaping lifestyle, with features of the arm bones pointing to some degree of brachiation (arm-swinging), have also been thrown into doubt.

Proconsul's skeletal features indicate that it was a remarkably generalised ape. It did not seem to have special adaptations for leaping from branch to trunk, or for swinging by its arms, or for walking on the ground. It probably moved quite slowly and cautiously in the trees, using its four limbs of equal length, and gripping with its strong hands and feet. It may well have come down to the ground and walked on all fours, though on the palms of its hands rather than "knuckle-walking" as in chimps and gorillas. Fossils and other evidence show the ecology: these species all lived in forests, although

THE FRONTAL SINUS

Sinuses are air spaces in the skull that are lined with mucous membrane. They are connected by openings to the air space inside the nose.

Humans have three pairs of sinuses. One pair is the frontal sinuses over the eyes, within the frontal bone. The frontal sinuses are interesting because they are a characteristic feature of humans and the African apes, the gorillas and chimps. They are lacking in the Asian *orangs, the lesser apes (gibbons), and other primates.*

Pronconsul also had frontal sinuses, of considerable size. This characteristic supports its close relationship to modern great apes and humans, rather than being out on its own limb of the phylogenetic tree.

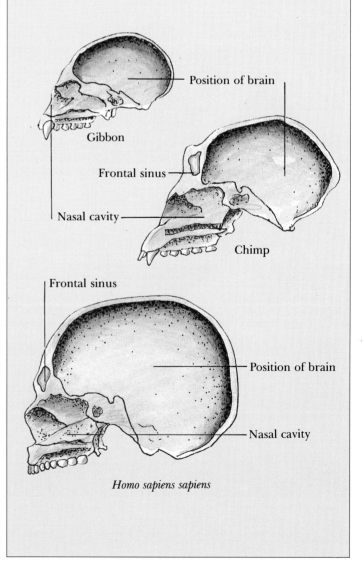

Gibbon — Position of brain

Frontal sinus

Nasal cavity

Chimp

Frontal sinus

Position of brain

Nasal cavity

Homo sapiens sapiens

TEETH, JAWS AND DIET

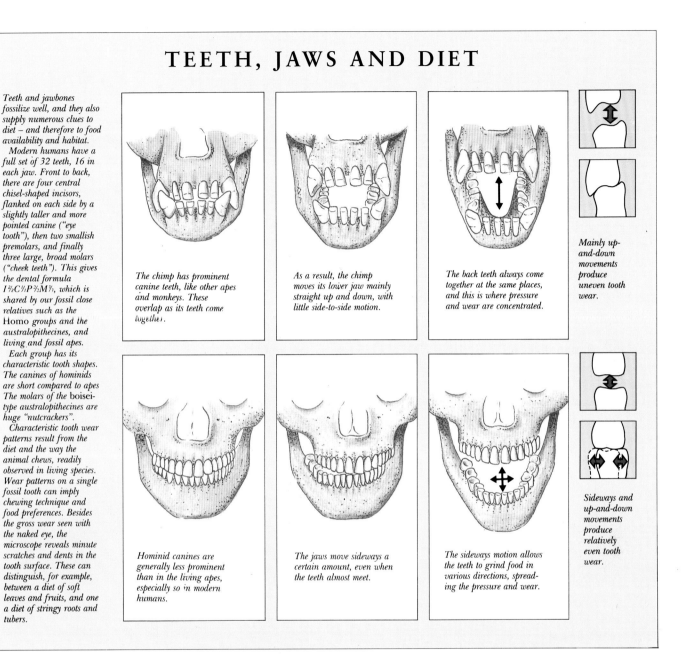

Teeth and jawbones fossilize well, and they also supply numerous clues to diet – and therefore to food availability and habitat.

Modern humans have a full set of 32 teeth, 16 in each jaw. Front to back, there are four central chisel-shaped incisors, flanked on each side by a slightly taller and more pointed canine ("eye tooth"), then two smallish premolars, and finally three large, broad molars ("cheek teeth"). This gives the dental formula $I\frac{2}{2}C\frac{1}{1}P\frac{2}{2}M\frac{3}{3}$, which is shared by our fossil close relatives such as the Homo groups and the australopithecines, and living and fossil apes.

Each group has its characteristic tooth shapes. The canines of hominids are short compared to apes. The molars of the boisei-type australopithecines are huge "nutcrackers".

Characteristic tooth wear patterns result from the diet and the way the animal chews, readily observed in living species. Wear patterns on a single fossil tooth can imply chewing technique and food preferences. Besides the gross wear seen with the naked eye, the microscope reveals minute scratches and dents in the tooth surface. These can distinguish, for example, between a diet of soft leaves and fruits, and one a diet of stringy roots and tubers.

The chimp has prominent canine teeth, like other apes and monkeys. These overlap as its teeth come together.

As a result, the chimp moves its lower jaw mainly straight up and down, with little side-to-side motion.

The back teeth always come together at the same places, and this is where pressure and wear are concentrated.

Mainly up-and-down movements produce uneven tooth wear.

Hominid canines are generally less prominent than in the living apes, especially so in modern humans.

The jaws move sideways a certain amount, even when the teeth almost meet.

The sideways motion allows the teeth to grind food in various directions, spreading the pressure and wear.

Sideways and up-and-down movements produce relatively even tooth wear.

Proconsul africanus may have frequented mixed woodland with open areas.

There are several views on Proconsul's relationships. Its generalised nature could mean that it resembles the common ancestor of modern-day great apes and humans. Yet its skeleton is a curious mosaic of ape-like and Old World monkey-like characteristics. Only a few features, such as possession of frontal sinuses, place it closer to the apes and humans, rather than the monkeys. Or the in-between nature of the evidence could indicate that Proconsul simply sits on its own distinct side branch of the great evolutionary tree.

APES IN EUROPE

Fossils of the ape known as Dryopithecus were first discovered in 1856, in southern France. They were two parts of the lower jaw. The creature was named after the dryads ("oak fairies"), since its remains were found with fossilised oak leaves.

Further discoveries in France, Austria, Germany, and Spain led to the naming of several dryopithecine species from this genus. The fossils are about 14–9 million years old, and like Sivapithecus, they are evidence for apes spreading out of Africa. For continental drift meant that

continued on page 42

DANGER IN THE UNDERGROWTH

When reconstructing the appearance and habits of a long-gone animal such as the Miocene ape *Dryopithecus*, fossil evidence is combined with a variety of other information, such as comparisons with similar prehistoric and present-day species. The remains of *Dryopithecus* are mostly bone fragments rather than whole bones, and they are scattered across widely separated geographical locations. After provisional identification, fossils from one site can be used to "fill in" missing parts from another, so building up a more complete version of the skeleton. At some sites, the fossils of plants and other animals in the same layers provide extra information. Evidence also comes from the types of sediments laid down, the regional location, and assumptions based on climates of today. The indications are that 10 million years ago, southern Europe was warmer than today, and mostly cloaked in mixed temperate and sub-tropical forests.

The various fossilised bone fragments and teeth of *Dryopithecus* show it was slightly smaller than a modern-day chimpanzee. (In certain circumstances, even a single tooth can be scaled up to give an approximate idea of the size of the whole animal.) The reassembled composite bones suggest limbs of roughly equal length, and grasping hands and feet, with a flat rather than a projecting doglike face. From such physical characteristics and its postulated habitat, we can guess that *Dryopithecus* probably moved easily among the branches. But its large size, bigger than most truly arboreal monkeys and apes of today, may have meant that it regularly came down to the ground.

The type of habitat and the various plant and animal fossils indicate food availability, and combine with details of the food-gathering and processing mechanisms of the animal itself – usually as indicated by its fossilised jaws and teeth – to give good clues to its diet. *Dryopithecus* probably ate fruit and other soft plant parts. However, the degree of bone reinforcement around the lower jaw, face and eyes implies a powerful chewing motion. Possibly *Dryopithecus* could also cope with tougher food such as nuts.

Dryopithecus *was larger than most truly tree-dwelling monkeys and apes of today. Its size may have made it a more formidable prey for hunters such as leopards. But it would also mean that* Dryopithecus *could not take refuge on the thinner, outer branches of a tree.*

Africa was previously an island, only coming into contact with Europe and Asia approximately 18 million years ago.

The fossils of *Dryopithecus* represent creatures similar in many respects to *Proconsul*, moving deliberately through the trees using all four limbs. (Some experts have renamed *Proconsul* as a member of the genus *Dryopithecus* as a result.) However, details of the arm bones and joints, and the presence of brow ridges over the eyes, place them fairly close in relationship to the modern great apes and humans.

APES IN ASIA

Fossils assigned to the hominoid genus *Sivapithecus* (some of which were, and still are, referred to as *Ramapithecus*) are about 13-7 million years old. They have been discovered in south-eastern Europe, Pakistan, and India. As a collection, they show great thickening of the enamel, especially on the molar teeth. Although mainly tree-dwelling, they were sizeable creatures and lived in more open types of woodland, so they may have descended frequently from the trees to the shrubby grassland below. The Miocene epoch was a time when the climate gradually cooled and became drier. Animals such as *Dryopithecus* in western Europe, and *Sivapithecus* in south-eastern Europe and Asia, would have found fewer trees and more grass.

Other characteristics of the face and the palate (the shelf of bone between nose and mouth) are shared by *Sivapithecus* and modern orangs, but not by other hominoids. Therefore opinion has swung around to regard *Sivapithecus* as probably a near relation of the orang, and not closely linked to the evolutionary lines of African great apes and humans.

Another Miocene ape with thickly enamelled teeth was *Gigantopithecus*. It resembled *Sivapithecus* in several respects, the main difference being size. *Gigantopithecus* was enormous. A big male stood over 8 feet tall and weighed up to 660 pounds – much bigger than a gorilla. It was first discovered in the 1930s to 1940s from teeth sold in traditional pharmacies in China, to be powdered into medicines.

More discoveries from India's Siwalik Hills indicate a *Gigantopithecus*-type creature could have been living there 8 million years ago. The most recent remains, from China, are apparently about 1 million years old. Most of the fossils are of teeth and jaws. Such limited

THE RAMAPITHECUS DEBATE

In the 1960s, a chief contender for one of our ancestors was Ramapithecus. *This hominoid was named after the Indian god Rama, for pieces of fossil jaw were discovered in 1932, in the Siwalik Hills of India's northern Kashmir province. They were dated at 12 million years old, and they implied human-like features such as a fairly flat face and jaws; a curved or parabolic lower jaw shape when viewed from above (ape lower jaws are more parallel-sided); small canine teeth; and no gap – the diastema – between the canine and incisor teeth in the upper jaw, into which would fit the large canine from the lower jaw.*

In the 1960s similar fossils, including parts of upper and lower jaws with teeth, came to prominence from Fort Ternan, Kenya. They were 14 million years old, and hailed as confirmation that Ramapithecus *was our direct and distant ancestor.*

In the 1970s, molecular studies began to point to a much more recent common ancestor of humans and today's great apes, putting the split at less than 10-7 million years ago. Experts on molecules argued with experts on fossils, and the status of Ramapithecus *looked doubtful.*

More Ramapithecus-*like fossils were found in Turkey, Pakistan and possibly China. They showed the animals had a more parallel-sided lower jaw, like other apes and unlike humans, and probably a diastema, too. Increasing evidence from molecular studies reinforced the idea of a recent split between humans and great apes.*

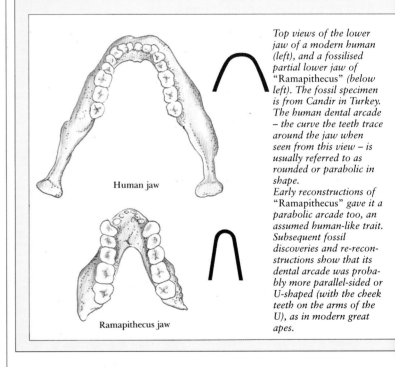

Human jaw

Ramapithecus jaw

Top views of the lower jaw of a modern human (left), and a fossilised partial lower jaw of "Ramapithecus" (below left). The fossil specimen is from Candir in Turkey. The human dental arcade – the curve the teeth trace around the jaw when seen from this view – is usually referred to as rounded or parabolic in shape.
Early reconstructions of "Ramapithecus" gave it a parabolic arcade too, an assumed human-like trait. Subsequent fossil discoveries and re-constructions show that its dental arcade was probably more parallel-sided or U-shaped (with the cheek teeth on the arms of the U), as in modern great apes.

evidence permits limited conclusions: *Gigantopithecus* was one of the many apes which evolved during the Miocene epoch, but its relationship with humans is unclear. However, it is fascinating to speculate that, because it may have survived until relatively recently, small and isolated groups of *Gigantopithecus* may have given rise to the legends of yetis, bigfoots, and similar creatures.

Oreopithecus is one of the best-known of Miocene fossil apes. It lived around 9–7 million years ago, and one almost complete but squashed fossil skeleton, plus

The resemblance of Ramapithecus teeth to those of Sivapithecus in all but size, became more apparent. Opinion has now swung away from the "special relationship" between Ramapithecus and the hominids. More fossil finds in the 1970s and 1980s have shown that the early reconstructions read too much into too few remains. Most newer studies refer to Ramapithecus chiefly to say that its fossils are now included under the name Sivapithecus.

The original "type specimen" fossils of Ramapithecus, from the Peabody Museum at Yale University, (left). Type specimens are the ones against which all subsequent finds are compared, to see if they should be included with the species in question, or be assigned to some other species, or even deserve a new species of their own. George Edward Lewis, discoverer of the first remains of Ramapithecus in 1932, is on the left in the newspaper cutting, with maps of the study area in northern India below.

numerous other remains, have been discovered in an area of Italy which would have been marshy swampland at the time. The swamp plants built up over millennia into lignite, which was being mined for fuel in the 1870s when the first *Oreopithecus* remains came to light.

Although *Oreopithecus* is so well known from fossils, there is little agreement about its significance to human evolution. Its skull and teeth are basically monkey-like, and indicate a folivorous (leafy) diet. Yet the rest of its skeleton has ape features, including the lack of a tail. The long arms have hands adapted as hooks for hang-ing from boughs, presumably so that the almost chimp-sized *Oreopithecus* could avoid descending to the pools and muddy ground below.

Oreopithecus remains a puzzle. Different views portray it as a strange relative of Old World monkeys; a side branch of the hominoid evolutionary tree, between the Old World monkeys and the apes/humans; or branching off after the gibbons and before the great apes and humans (page 35). The many remains of *Oreopithecus* encourage as much discussion and lack of firm conclusions, as those animals known from only a few scrappy fragments.

THE "LATE MIOCENE GAP"

Towards the end of the Miocene epoch, there is a missing chapter in the hominoid fossil record. From about 8 million years ago, until after 4 million years ago, there are virtually no well-documented remains of apes or (as yet) humans, anywhere in the world. Isolated teeth and fragments of possibly hominoid jaws, skull, arm, and leg bones have been recovered in Kenya and Libya. But there can be no firm conclusions from such scarce remains. One factor is the scarcity of fossil-bearing rocks from land sediments; most of the fossils are of sea creatures in sea-bed sediments.

This time period is known as the "late Miocene gap." The previously numerous and diverse Miocene apes, described above, fade quickly from the scene. This means there are no fossils to reveal the origins of the gorilla and chimp, either. Molecular studies provide the data in this area (page 25).

When the record resumes, the next chapter in our own history opens not with fossils again, but with footprints.

OREOPITHECUS

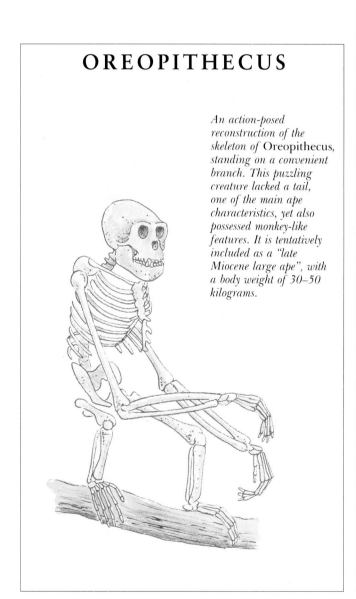

An action-posed reconstruction of the skeleton of Oreopithecus, *standing on a convenient branch. This puzzling creature lacked a tail, one of the main ape characteristics, yet also possessed monkey-like features. It is tentatively included as a "late Miocene large ape", with a body weight of 30–50 kilograms.*

OUR CLOSEST LIVING RELATIVES

For more than a century, anatomical studies have placed the great apes – gorillas, chimps, and orangs – in one group, with humans in another, closely-related group (page 35). In the past 20 years, evidence from molecular structure and behavioural research has added a new perspective to the question: which are our closest living relatives?

Anatomy and morphology
Chimps and gorillas are similar to each other, and different from humans, in these features:

● they move on all fours, often by knuckle-walking;
● they live partly in trees, swinging from the branches; their legs are shorter, and arms longer;
● their hands are designed to bear weight, both when branch-hanging and knuckle-walking, and are less flexible and manipulative;
● their brains are smaller;
● their canine teeth are larger; they have thin enamel on their molar teeth;
● their bodies are covered with longer hair.

The conclusion here is that chimps and gorillas are most closely related to each other, and then both are fairly closely related to humans.

Molecules and genes
The data from studies of body molecules, including the "blueprint of life," DNA, show that:

● humans, chimps, and gorillas are 99 percent similar in their genes (there is a gap between these three species and the orang);

● gene sequencing for molecules involved in the immune system shows humans and chimps share the most similarities;

● research on DNA in the mitochondria of each cell

(explained in Chapter Seven) gives the same result, with humans and chimps most similar;

● a technique called DNA hybridisation, which takes single strands of DNA from two species and assesses how well they fit together, shows likewise.

The conclusion here is that humans and chimps are most closely related to each other.

Behaviour
It is not yet possible to analyse behaviour in a quantifiable way, on a scale of points or numbers. However, observations in the wild show that:

● chimps form small parties and larger communities, and have a much more fluid and complex social life than gorillas;

● chimps use tools, which gorillas rarely do;

● chimps band together and act aggressively, toward other animals and to their own kind; in chimp hunting parties, individuals regularly take the same roles, such as drivers, chasers, ambushers, or prey-dismemberers – the only species known to have such a specialised degree of teamwork other than humans;

● very recent studies revealed a mother chimp "teaching" her offspring, demonstrating how to hold and use a stone to break awkward bits of food.

It seems that humans and chimps share certain more complex behaviour patterns not shown by gorillas, but there are great differences in the degree of development.

The overall conclusion
Morphology and molecules disagree – or rather, interpretations of what they mean disagree. The trend has been toward accepting that the common chimpanzee, rather than chimps and gorillas together, may be our closest living relative.

(Below) A gorilla holds a worn bough in what could be a threatening posture as a weapon about to strike. At the time, however, the animal was simply manipulating the wood in random positions, occasionally sniffing it or rubbing its face. Unlike chimps, gorillas use tools only rarely.

THE
SOUTHERN
APES

On September 15, 1976, a biologist playfully threw a lump of dried elephant dung at a palaeontologist. They were near the camp at Laetoli, 25 miles south of Olduvai Gorge, in northern Tanzania. The famous palaeontologist Louis Leakey had visited the area in the 1930s, and a team had returned in 1974 with his wife Mary, to renew the search for fossils and our origins. As the palaeontologist, Andrew Hill, ducked to avoid the missile, he stumbled and noticed that the hard surface beneath his feet was covered with tiny indentations. Closer inspection identified them as the fossilized pockmarks made by raindrops hitting a once-soft surface. Looking around, he recognised fossilised animal tracks, too. He had fallen onto the bed of a dried-up watercourse and found it to be a "pavement" covered in animal prints.

Before the work season finished for that year, careful excavations uncovered the preserved tracks of elephants, rhinos, hares, and birds. They provided valuable evidence of the creatures living in the ecological community more than 3 million years ago.

ANIMAL HIGHWAYS

In July 1978, in the continuing search at Laetoli, Paul Abell found half a print which anatomist Michael Day identified as "human-like." With great care and mount-

ing excitement the excavations continued into 1979. Finally an amazing trail of fossilised human-like footprints was revealed, dated since at just over 3.6 million years old. The scientists at the camp had regularly walked over this patch of ground on their way to the main fossil-bearing rocks nearby. They were not the first creatures to walk with a two-legged striding gait across the landscape. Further work identified the tracks of guinea fowl, hares, antelopes, gazelles, the extinct three-toed horse, hyenas, pigs, giraffes, elephants, and rhinos.

The tracks had been preserved in the following way. Some 3.6–3.7 million years ago a nearby volcano, Mount Sadiman, had showered the area with eruptions of light volcanic ash. Subsequent showers of rain wetted the ash so that it would take the prints of creatures wandering to and fro. Then the ash dried and baked in the African sun, with the prints intact. Chemicals in the volcanic ash had reacted with the rainwater to make a type of "cement" which set hard.

This process happened several times, with each new shower protecting the already-hard tracks beneath, and producing six or more distinct layers of fossilised volcanic ash, about 6 inches (15 centimetres) thickness in total.

Two footprint trails, which can be followed for some 165 feet (50 metres), would be difficult to distinguish from your own footprints as you walk along a beach of

With her fossilized skeleton about 40 percent complete, "Lucy" was one of the most amazing finds in the search for our origins. She showed that the evolution of upright walking preceded the evolution of a bigger brain – contrary to the expectations of many scientists. Her kind are usually known as Australopithecus afarensis.

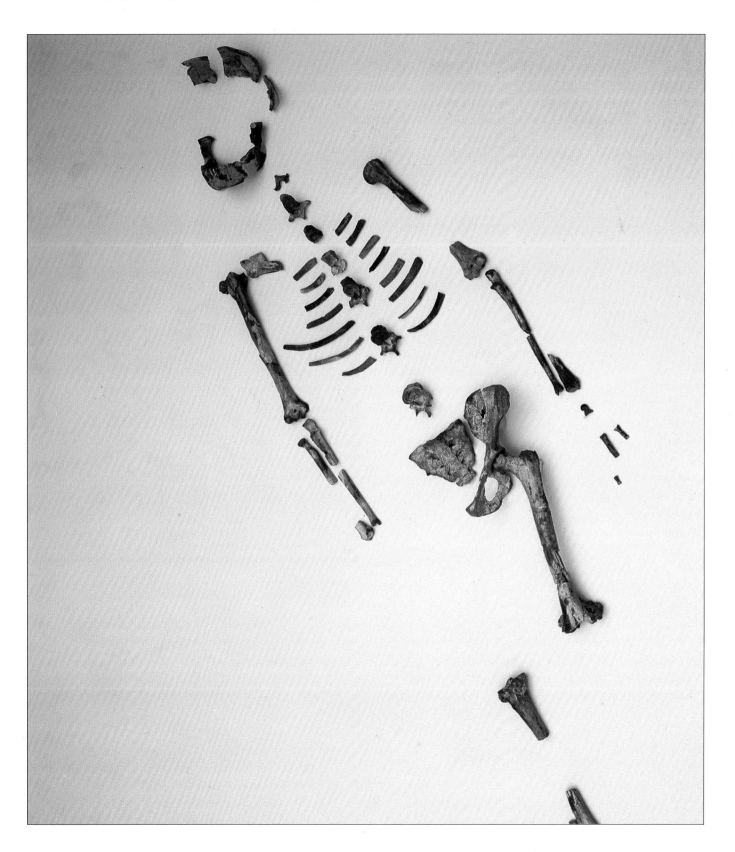

damp sand. Calculations from their foot size and stride (distance apart) show that they were made by two individuals, the larger around 55 inches (1.4 metre) tall, the other some 8 inches (20 centimetres) shorter.

WHO MADE THE FOOTPRINTS?

The trails are about 10 inches (25 centimetres) apart. This is too close for the creatures to have been walking side by side. Possibly one was just in front. In places it seems that a third set of prints is superimposed within the large ones. It is as though a third individual had stepped in the tracks of the large one – as when children, playing on the beach, walk in each other's footprints. Differences in the sharpness and "give" of the damp ash indicate that the different trails could have been made at different times. Nevertheless, it is tempting to view the Laetoli footprints as evidence of a family out for a walk, 3.6 million years ago, looking for food or water, or fleeing to escape the volcano's rumblings.

The prints are remarkably human. Analysis of their shape shows that the big toe lay alongside the other toes, and was only slightly longer than them – not considerably longer, and splayed at an angle, as in the apes. The deepest parts of the prints are on the ball and heel; the areas of least indentation are in the arch and along the outer edge of the foot. This pattern of weight distribution is almost exactly the same as in a footprint of a modern human walking along. It indicates a two-legged, striding type of walk, rather than the "rolling gait" of a creature that rarely walks on two legs, such as the chimp.

It is interesting to note that, whoever made the prints, the traces they left are more conclusive than finding their actual fossils instead. The shapes of bones imply how their owners stood and moved, but these implications are open to "discussion" and "interpretation." Compared to form, function is more direct evidence. No one can seriously deny that the footprints show upright walking was well evolved by 3.6 million years ago.

Fossilised hominid teeth and bones, including lower jaws and parts of skeletons, were also found at Laetoli. They show a degree of similarity to remains uncovered at several sites in Africa, including Hadar in Ethiopia. The exact "degree of similarity" has been at the root of much disagreement among the experts, and is discussed further on page 64. Overall, the evidence suggests the footprints were made by creatures known as australop-

Henry Fairfield Osborn, director of the American Museum of Natural History at the time of Dart's discovery, was dismissive of the claims for the Taung skull. Osborn and many of his colleagues believed that human origins would be found in Asia, and his museum sent several expeditions to the Gobi Desert area in eastern Asia in the 1920s. They found wonderful dinosaur fossils, including eggs, but no human or pre-human remains.

ithecines – whose fossils had first been uncovered 50 years earlier, and who have been the subject of great debate ever since.

STRANGE FINDS IN SOUTH AFRICA

"The specimen is of importance because it exhibits an extinct race of apes intermediate between living anthropoids and man." So wrote Raymond Dart in the preliminary report on a fossil skull from South Africa. The report was published in the science journal Nature on February 7, 1925. He named the type of creature whose

Photographed in his later years, Raymond Dart (left) cradles the Taung skull, which he discovered at the age of 32. He was immensely satisfied at its final acceptance by the scientific community, after two decades of its denial. Almost the entire face of this young australopithecine child has been preserved virtually intact

The Taung fossil lacked bony ridges above the eyes; its face was relatively flat; and the jaws did not jut forwards as much as in an adult ape. In fact the jaws had first or "milk" teeth. The second (permanent or adult) set of molar teeth were just coming through. It was the remains of a youngster, perhaps five or six at the age of death. (This age has since been revised, on the basis of enamel layering, to nearer three years.)

The canines were small, and apart from the slightly larger size of the molars, the teeth were human-like including the pattern of cusps ("bumps") on the grinding surface of each back tooth. The cusp pattern of the first molar tooth was particularly similar to the human pattern.

The foramen magnum was also interesting. This is the hole in the skull where the base of the brain narrows into the spinal column and passes out of the skull, into the spine. In the Taung skull it was positioned approximately underneath, rather than towards the back. This indicated the creature's skull balanced on top of its spine, instead of the spine joining the skull more horizontally from behind, as in an ape with an all-fours posture. It implied that *Australopithecus africanus* stood upright.

remains were represented by the fossil as *Australopithecus africanus*, or "southern ape from Africa."

The small skull in question had been blasted from a lime quarry near Taung, not far from the famous Kimberley diamond mines, in the previous year. The fossil was sent to Dart, who was Professor of Anatomy at Witwatersrand University, Johannesburg. Dart cleaned away the surrounding rock to reveal the remains of a small but almost complete face and lower jaw, with teeth, and the right side of the braincase. Rock had formed inside the right part of the braincase, taking on the shape of the original contents as it did so to form an endocast.

During his training, Dart had studied under the Professor of Anatomy at University College in London, Grafton Elliot Smith. He knew of Smith's theory that the gap between a certain pair of fissures (the deep grooves covering the brain) was much smaller in apes than in humans. The Taung endocast had a largish gap between the fissures.

Dart also proposed that contours of the cast indicated the brain was larger than that of a comparable ape, and that it was of "improved quality," with certain key parts well developed. He proposed that the creature could probably see colours, appreciate sounds, and be capable of some degree of articulate speech.

CRANIAL ENDOCASTS

The natural stone filling of the inside cavity of a fossil bone is known as an endocast. The endocast may remain long after the original bone, and even its fossil, have disappeared. Endocasts provide valuable evidence about the shape of the soft parts which occupied the cavity in life.

A rock cast of the interior of the skull, using the cranium as its mold, is a cranial endocast (or endocranial cast). It is not strictly a "brain cast," since in life the brain does not touch the inside of the bone. It is covered by three membranes, the meninges, with fluid layers sandwiched between them. Nevertheless, allowances can be made for these, so that it is possible to work back and calculate the brain's approximate volume and contours.

NO MISSING LINK

The find caused a whirlwind of publicity. Popular newspapers announced MISSING LINK NO LONGER MISSING and MISSING LINK THAT COULD SPEAK. First estimates gave the fossils an age of 5 million years. But the scientific community was not convinced. It was at first politely non-committal, then sceptical, and eventually derisive, as described below.

It is now accepted that the Taung skull was the first scientifically recognised specimen of the group known as the australopithecines. Like us, they are classified as hominids, in our family Hominidae. Dozens of subsequent finds have confirmed and expanded Dart's conclusions, and somewhere among the australopithecines may be our direct ancestors. With the benefit of hindsight, why was the Taung find rejected in the 1920s, and virtually ignored for another 20 years?

Several eminent anthropologists examined casts of the fossil when these became available. Most judged that the skull was not human or even prehuman, but from a small chimp or gorilla. Its young age served to confuse matters. Dart's report was supposed to contain an impartial and objective description, but it emphasised the human-like features, while diminishing the apelike ones. Other anthropologists reacted against this and did the opposite, ascribing apparently human traits to the tender age of the owner at death.

Moreover, the fossil's non-human brain volume but human-like teeth did not fit into the picture of human evolution which was then favoured. An enlarged brain was seen as the first, vital human characteristic to evolve. Other features, such as bipedal walking and smaller teeth and jaws, would then trail along in its

Robert Broom, one of Dart's few supporters, spent many hours on his hands and knees in the Transvaal limestone caves of South Africa, probing for "apeman" fossils. Below left, he examines closely a find at Swartkrans.

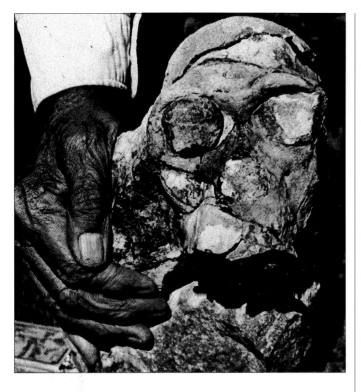

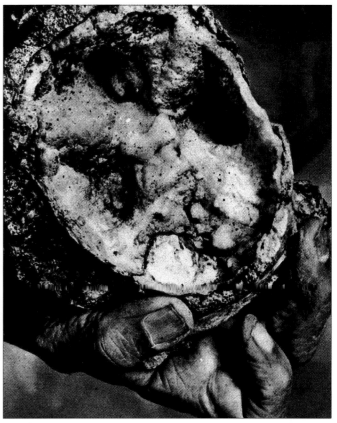

The sequence of photographs (opposite and left) chronicles Broom's discovery of the famously complete Australopithecus Sterkfontein *skull on April 18, 1947. The fossil was in two pieces when found, and Broom points to a lower portion (opposite, above). A side view after its partial removal shows the base still embedded in the rock (opposite, below right). The front view reveals the eyebrow ridges and flattened braincase (above). Seen from below, the inside of the braincase is clearly visible (Right).*

wake. An early human ancestor should therefore have a large brain, but its jaws and other parts should be primitive and apelike – features shown uncannily well by the Piltdown fossils, found a decade earlier (page 36).

What was more, the time between the fossil coming into Dart's hands, and his first report in the scientific press, was an exceptionally short six weeks. Surely he could not have taken sufficient time to study the skull thoroughly, analyse its features accurately, and debate their significance with learned colleagues? The scientific establishment usually pondered over reports like these for years, and preferably in a scholarly centre such as London, not in faraway South Africa where academic resources and specimens for comparison were so limited.

Also, the location of the find contradicted the notion then prevalent that the first true humans evolved in Asia. At the time of the Taung find, several expeditions were being undertaken to places such as China and Mongolia, with the aim of discovering our ancestors.

Eugene Dubois in Java had directed attention there at the end of the 19th century (Chapter Five). In the 1920s more discoveries from Choukoutien, China, kept eastern Asia in the spotlight. In 1921 Richard Lull, Yale University's Professor of Anthropology, stated: "That Asia is the birthplace of mankind is seemingly established." It seemed that Africa was just not "noble" enough to be the cradle of mankind.

In the face of such resistance, Dart and the Taung fossil faded from public attention. The remains, and the animal they came from, were unkindly christened "Dart's baby." As with the Neandertal saga of 50 years previously, human preconception and prejudice played its part in the "objective interpretation" of the evidence.

BROOM AND TAUNG'S REHABILITATION

Robert Broom was one of Dart's few firm supporters. A medical doctor, he had studied marsupial fossils in Australia, and was a world expert on the remains of mammal-like reptiles, which lived before and alongside the dinosaurs, in South Africa. He soon examined the Taung skull and, almost alone among his peers, decided that Dart's interpretation was correct.

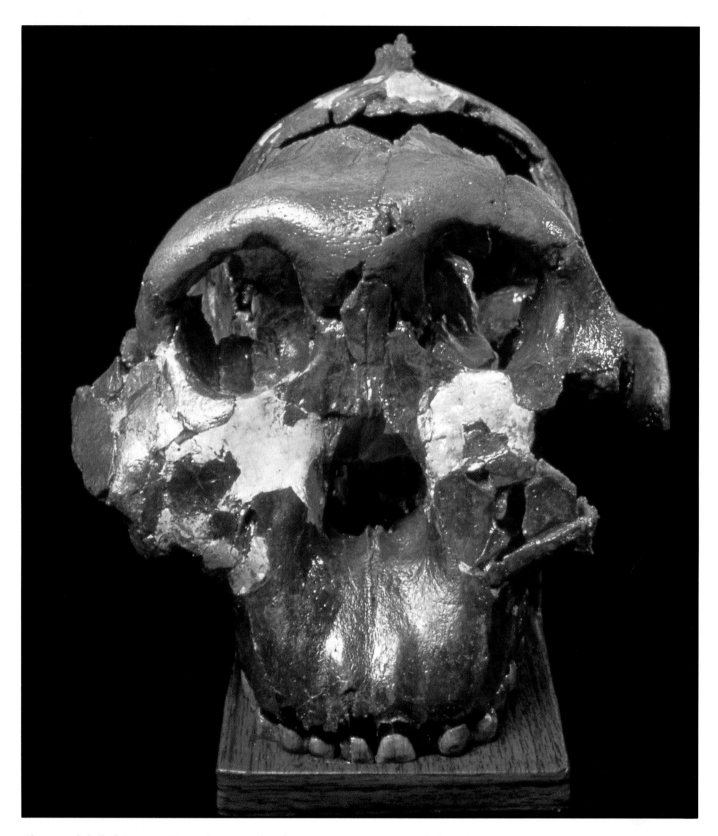

The restored skull of "Zinj" or "Nutcracker Man", the robust australopithecine discovered at Olduvai Gorge in East Africa by Mary Leakey, in 1959. The braincase is relatively small, but the cheekbones or zygomatic arches are enormous, as are the back teeth. The whole skull is more solidly built than the robust australopithecines from South Africa. The find was initially nicknamed "Dear Boy" by the Leakeys.

Dart and Broom separated the lower and upper jaws of the Taung "ape-child" in 1929. They saw at once that the teeth were even more human than had been supposed. The two doctors also discussed the environment at the time, agreeing that the Taung countryside would have been dry and peppered with caves, where australopithecines could have lived. In the caves were fossils of at least a dozen kinds of mammal, including antelopes, small baboons, springhares, burrowing rodents, and dassies, as well as remains of lizards, tortoises, and crabs.

Later, Dart and Broom were to propose that the australopithecines may have used weapons of bones, antlers, and teeth – the first tools – to kill and dismember these prey animals. But the evidence is now regarded as slight. Instead, the caves full of remains may have been the caches of large carnivores such as leopards, with the australopithecines as the hunted rather than hunters. Or the various bodies could have been washed into the caves during floods. Even so, many of the species represented are now extinct, and Dart and Broom tentatively dated the Taung fossils at around 2 million years old.

MORE "SOUTH AFRICAN APE-MEN"

Broom took the post of Curator of Vertebrate Palaeontology and Physical Anthropology at the Transvaal Museum, Pretoria. In 1936 he began excavations at Sterkfontein, near the gold-boom town of Krugersdorp. After only three months he had discovered the fossilised cranial endocast, skull base, upper jaw and braincase fragments of another australopithecine-type creature, which he dated provisionally at 1.2 million years old. Broom felt it differed sufficiently from the Taung specimen to be given not only a separate species but also a separate genus, so he named its kind *Plesianthropus transvaalensis* – "near-man of the Transvaal." (It is now assigned to *Australopithecus africanus*.)

In 1938, with the help of a local schoolboy, Broom came upon some teeth, lower right jaw and left part of a skull from a prehistoric cave at Kromdraai, about two miles from Sterkfontein. These showed a hominid with a heavier build, and more powerful jaws and teeth, than the other Australopithecus-type remains. Approximate dating was 800,000 years old. Broom created not only another new species but yet another new genus,

Bones, fossils, and the excavation site and working area at Makapansgat (below), another of the South African sites, some 200 miles north of Johannesburg. Some of the australopithecines found there in the 1940s were called Australopithecus prometheus *by Raymond Dart, in the belief that they used fire. This interpretation is no longer accepted.*

Paranthropus robustus or "robust near-man."

In 1946 Broom and his co-workers published *The South African Fossil Ape-Men*, complete with full descriptions and photographs. There was a mass of evidence that two main kinds of australopithecines had once lived there: the smaller, lightly built "gracile" types, and the bigger, more heavily built, thicker-boned "robust" types (page 63).

A problem was that many of the remains came from prehistoric caves and were embedded in breccias – rocks consisting mainly of a mixture of angular fragments, which had not long been broken from their own parent rocks. These mixed accumulations were notoriously difficult to date, one of the few methods being comparative dating using fossils of other animals associated with the hominid remains. But the scientific community could no longer ignore the matter, and took up study and debate in earnest.

In the same year at Sterkfontein, Broom found an amazingly complete australopithecine skull, from a female, and a male lower jaw. Then a vital piece of evidence – a pelvis, or hip bone. Its dimensions were so different from those of a chimp or gorilla that its owner almost certainly walked upright. More and more fossils came to light. South Africa and the australopithecines were truly on the map.

Many australopithecine fossils have since been found, improving our knowledge of these creatures immensely. But the current situation regarding their classification might be termed "fluid," or "unresolved." There are still areas of uncertainty and heated debate among the

Mary Leakey (right) views the plaque in honor of "Zinj," at the site where she unearthed the fossil.

A photograph of Robert Broom heads a collection of sketches, notes, newspaper reports, and his drafts for scientific reports (below).

experts. Maybe there are simply not enough fossils available, as yet, to make firm conclusions. It helps to understand the contexts of further recent discoveries, before discussing questions such as: How many kinds or species of australopithecines were there? When, where, and how did they live? And were any of them our direct ancestors?

"NUTCRACKER MAN"

Olduvai Gorge is probably the world's best-known fossil site. It is a deep ravine-like valley in northern Tanzania, towards the east of the Serengeti plains, and part of the great African Rift Valley system. In places the broken cliffs tumble almost 330 feet down to the floor, where only occasionally the river that cuts the gorge flows.

Fossils were originally found at Olduvai by a butterfly collector. They have been excavated for most of this century, commencing with Hans Reck, the German palaeontologist, in 1913. Twelve years later Louis Leakey, a son of English missionary parents, himself born in Africa, saw Reck's specimens and decided to search the gorge. By the early 1930s, Leakey was organising fossil-hunting expeditions, and he was soon joined by his wife, Mary.

During the following two decades, the Leakeys found thousands of animal fossils, and also hundreds of stone tools. The tools were mostly unsophisticated but undoubtably effective.

In 1959 Mary Leakey came upon a major find. It was a fairly complete australopithecine-type skull, thick-boned, heavily-built, and generally "robust." The type of creature it represented was christened *Zinjanthropus boisei*, "Boise's Man from East Africa," after Zinj, an Arabic name for East Africa, and Charles Boise, who funded the expeditions. The creature was known more informally as Zinj, or "Nutcracker Man" in the popular

press, on account of its enormous back teeth. It is now considered to be a robust australopithecine (page 63).

Zinj was one of the first hominid specimens to be subjected to radiodating. Initial estimates from the geology of the site were around 600,000 years. Radiodating gave almost 1.8 million years old. This surprisingly ancient date spurred the Leakeys and other palaeontologists to fresh searches. It was suggested that Zinj and his people may have made the stone scrapers and cutters found at Olduvai – tools of a type termed the Oldowan culture, named by Leakey after the gorge itself. However, it is now thought that *Homo habilis*, whose fossils also occur at Olduvai, was the likely tool-maker (Chapter Four).

EXPEDITIONS TO HADAR

During the 1960s, many exciting discoveries were made in East Africa, at Olduvai and other sites. Then in the 1970s attention shifted dramatically far to the north, to the Afar region in northeastern Ethiopia, and south to the Laetoli footprints described previously.

Donald Johanson, an American anthropologist, had made a detailed study of chimp teeth for his Master's degree. In 1973 he joined an international expedition to the Afar region. Surveys of the gorges cut by the Hadar river system, and the fossils these exposed, suggested the sediments were laid down as long ago as 4 million years. This predated many other sites. If hominid remains were found at Hadar, they would be the oldest yet discovered.

In 1973 Johanson visited French geologist Maurice Taieb and the French anthropologist Yves Coppens, along with members of the Ethiopian Antiquities Department, on the first expedition. They had set up base camp on the banks of the (in the wet season) fast-flowing, aptly-named Awash River. Months of work yielded several thousand fossils, but only four hominid ones - pieces of leg bone. Even so, two of the fragments seemed to fit together to produce a knee joint adapted for upright walking. These remains were more than 3 million years old.

In the autumn of 1974, various teeth and jawbones were uncovered, showing a mixture of ape and human features. One fossilised palate had 16 teeth in place. An announcement from the team stated: "We have ... extended our knowledge of the genus *Homo* by nearly 1.5 million years. All previous theories of the origins of the lineage which leads to modern man must now be totally revised." More than 3 million years ago, "the genus *Homo* was walking, eating meat and probably using tools to kill animals ..."

However many palaeoanthropologists reserved judgement. The fossils showed some australopithecine traits, and some human ones, but there was no indication of brain capacity. Surely evidence of a large brain was needed, to include the fossils in the genus *Homo*? More evidence was soon forthcoming, but of a very different nature.

"LUCY" COMES TO LIGHT

On Christmas Eve, 1974, Johanson and his colleague Tom Gray found a piece of hominid arm bone jutting from an anonymous-looking rocky slope at Hadar. Then other pieces were identified, and soon they realised they had a tremendous find – a partial skeleton. After another three weeks of searching, about two-fifths of a female hominid skeleton were recovered.

It was one of the most remarkable finds in the search for our origins. Officially catalogued as AL 288-1 Partial Skeleton, its kind were scientifically named in 1978 as *Australopithecus afarensis* – "southern ape from Afar". (This name fuelled a great controversy at the time.) But she is more famously known to the world at large as "Lucy," after the Beatles song *Lucy in the Sky with Diamonds*, which was then a camp favourite on the taperecorder.

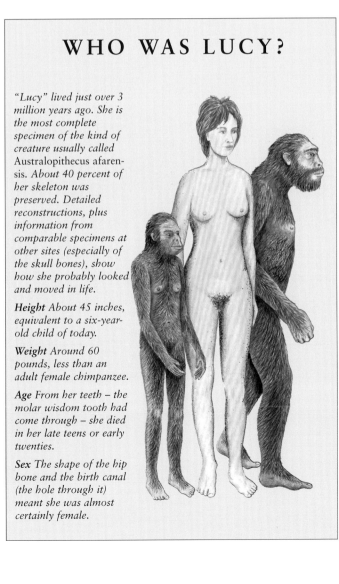

WHO WAS LUCY?

"Lucy" lived just over 3 million years ago. She is the most complete specimen of the kind of creature usually called Australopithecus afarensis. *About 40 percent of her skeleton was preserved. Detailed reconstructions, plus information from comparable specimens at other sites (especially of the skull bones), show how she probably looked and moved in life.*

Height *About 45 inches, equivalent to a six-year-old child of today.*

Weight *Around 60 pounds, less than an adult female chimpanzee.*

Age *From her teeth – the molar wisdom tooth had come through – she died in her late teens or early twenties.*

Sex *The shape of the hip bone and the birth canal (the hole through it) meant she was almost certainly female.*

This range of hominids displays specimens discovered by Richard Leakey and his team at the East Turkana site in Kenya, around 1968–72. The two skulls on the right are typical of the heavily built robust australopithecines, with great flanges on the cheekbones. The larger male skull is in front of the smaller female one. Second from the left is a gracile australopithecine, showing its much lighter facial bones compared to the robust cousins. On the far left is a specimen of Homo erectus *(see Chapter 5), a more recent hominid and possibly our direct ancestor, displaying its bigger braincase and less jutting upper jaw.*

THE "FIRST FAMILY"

The following year, 1975, Johanson and his colleagues came upon the remains of the "First Family" – a collection of fossils making up at least 13 hominid individuals, a mixture of infants, children and adults, males and females. They date from more than 3 million years ago, and indicated creatures much bigger than Lucy, with a combination of modern and primitive features.

At first sight the "Family" seemed to have died together. There are various explanations for the close proximity of this collection of ribs, vertebrae, leg bones, hand and foot bones, jaws, teeth, and skull fragments. Did a flash flood sweep the group to their death as they slept? Or did they fall ill and die from an epidemic of disease? Or had the bones collected coincidentally at the same spot over some years. Perhaps a stream washed them there. Or a carnivore such as a leopard dropped the remains of its hominid victims one by one, from its branch into a water-hole below, where they fossilized in the mud.

WALKING ON TWO LEGS

Some decades ago, it was believed that the evolution of two-legged walking in early hominids tied in neatly with large brains and tools. As the brain became bigger and more "intelligent," the hands were used increasingly for manipulation, tool-using, and tool-making; and less for moving with all four limbs, through the branches or on the ground. Freed from a weight-bearing and propulsive role in locomotion, the hands became increasingly dexterous and manipulative.

The discovery of the Laetoli footprints, and fossils of individuals such as Lucy, changed this view. They showed that creatures that still resembled apes in some respects – especially brain size – were already standing upright and walking on two legs, almost 4 million years ago. This is well over 1 million years before the earliest evidence of stone tools. Presumably these creatures had already gone through an evolutionary transition, which would push back the beginnings of bipedalism still further.

So why did bipedalism appear? Evolutionary theory would say it must have had some advantage. Several advantages have been postulated, but no single one seems to outweigh the others. Perhaps several factors were at work.

The initial impetus may well have been environmental change. As the climate continued to become drier through the Miocene epoch, forests with extensive canopies that needed moisture were replaced by more drought-resistant open woodland and savanna grassland. The ability to move easily over the ground, rather than swing through the branches, would have been advantageous. An upright posture would help to give a better view of the surroundings. A small creature on four legs cannot see very far in long grass. Standing up on two legs enables it to see over the grass, in the search for food and predators. Some savannah animals today, such as baboons, occasionally stand upright when on "lookout." But then they drop on all-fours again. Could this factor have been so powerful at the time that the early hominids had to walk tall as well as stand tall?

Another proposal is that walking enabled these early hominids to carry something – food, babies, or as-yet-unknown tools, weapons, or other items. Perhaps they gathered armfuls of food and carried them to others in their group (presuming they lived in groups and shared food), or to some kind of home base. Perhaps they carried their young in their arms as they travelled quickly after food on the hoof. They may have strode after the great game herds on the savannah, picking off stragglers or scavenging on carcasses. Bipedalism is highly suited to the energy-conserving "dogged pursuit" style of hunting, moving in the way that we would call jogging today. However, evidence from the microscopic wear patterns on fossil teeth indicate that those early hominids ate mainly fruit and plant materials, and only small quantities of meat, rather like chimps and baboons today. Wear patterns suggesting a diet with appreciable amounts of meat do not appear until nearer 2 million years ago (around the time of the first tools).

Another intriguing proposal concerns not behaviour, but physiology: body temperature control. As the forest's leafy shade dwindled, exposure to the searing heat of the African sun increased. While some parts of the body can tolerate a certain amount of overheating, others, especially the brain, cannot. Standing upright could have helped. First, it reduced the area of the body which absorbed heat, especially in the overhead midday sun. Scale models show that an upright biped absorbs less than half of the sun's radiation than an equivalent-sized, all-fours quadruped. Second, it would raise more of the body above the surrounding vegetation, to be cooled by the breeze. A head of hair would be usefully retained, to

Donald Johanson (in the blue shirt) and his co-workers behind their collection of fossils from the Hadar River ravines and tributary valleys in the Afar region of Ethiopia.

shield the top of the skull and the sensitive brain from the sun's strongest rays. Meanwhile a hairy covering over the rest of the body would be usefully reduced, to allow the breeze to pass over the skin and evaporate sweat, thereby promoting the cooling effect.

AUSTRALOPITHECINES AROUND AFRICA

Along with the Taung baby, Olduvai's Zinj, and Hadar's Lucy and First Family, early hominid fossils have been found at various sites in Africa. Many of these are included in the australopithecine group. But other discoveries are more debatable.

At Koobi Fora in northern Kenya, a number of Zinj-like and other remains have been discovered (see below); and at Natron in Tanzania, a jawbone of the Zinj kind was discovered by Richard Leakey. Besides the footprints, Laetoli has yielded a number of australopithecine or other early hominid fossils.

From Omo in Ethiopia come hundreds of early hominid fragments (as well as some larger parts and skulls). Their identification is uncertain. But the plentiful fossils of other creatures such as pigs, rodents and antelopes, plus layers of volcanic rocks which can be subjected to absolute dating, make the Omo evidence very useful for relative dating (page 25).

And there are the numerous finds made by Broom and others, from the South African cave deposits at Sterkfontein, Kromdraai, Swartkrans, and Makapansgat.

THE SOUTH AFRICAN HOMINIDS

Is there a current consensus concerning the different kinds of australopithecines, and where and when they lived? As mentioned previously, the situation is "fluid." The South African early hominids seem to fall into two main groups: the slimmer, smaller, slender "graciles," and the bigger, beefier "robusts."

The former are usually known by the name *Australopithecus africanus*, originally given by Dart to the Taung skull. In life, these creatures were about 50 inches tall and 75 pounds in weight (similar to a healthy ten-year-old child of today). The brain size was 450–550 milliliters, comparable to a chimp. They may have lived about 3–2 million years ago. No skeletons have been found that are anywhere near as complete as Lucy, but in general, *Australopithecus africanus* seems to have been less ape-like than *Australopithecus afarensis*, its East African cousin (see below), with bigger teeth to cope with tougher foods. It did not have the ape-like bony ridges on its skull, and its face was flatter, with less projecting jaws.

It is believed that *Australopithecus africanus* males were larger than the females, as in chimps and gorillas, and as in modern humans, though to a much less marked degree. This is a feature termed sexual dimorphism, a recurrent theme in many debates on hominid evolution. It means that within a species, members of one sex are on average significantly different from members of the other sex, in terms of a physical feature such as height, size, muscle development or bone shape (excluding, of course, the usual differences in the sexual organs).

The bigger, more powerful australopithecines from South Africa are usually regarded as a different species, and even a separate genus, from the gracile

continued on page 62

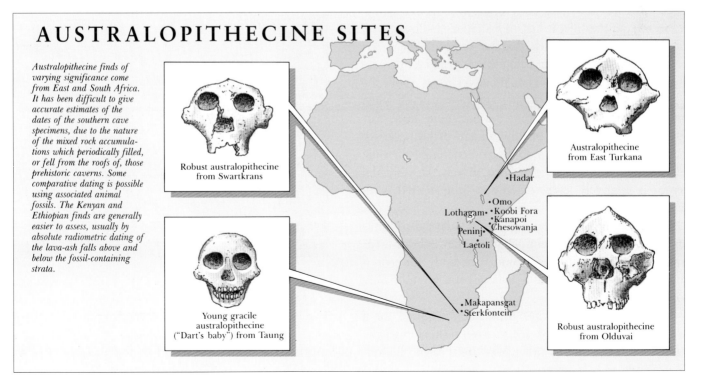

AUSTRALOPITHECINE SITES

Australopithecine finds of varying significance come from East and South Africa. It has been difficult to give accurate estimates of the dates of the southern cave specimens, due to the nature of the mixed rock accumulations which periodically filled, or fell from the roofs of, those prehistoric caverns. Some comparative dating is possible using associated animal fossils. The Kenyan and Ethiopian finds are generally easier to assess, usually by absolute radiometric dating of the lava-ash falls above and below the fossil-containing strata.

Robust australopithecine from Swartkrans

Young gracile australopithecine ("Dart's baby") from Taung

Australopithecine from East Turkana

Robust australopithecine from Olduvai

•Hadar
•Omo
Lothagam• •Koobi Fora
Peninj• •Kanapoi
•Chesowanja
Laetoli

•Makapansgat
•Sterkfontein

TWO-LEGGED WALKING

Adopting an upright posture and bipedal gait was associated with profound changes in the hominid skeleton and musculature, compared to the basic ape-like design. However, parts of the basic primate body can be seen as "pre-adapted" to bipedalism. For example, many other primates, from bushbabies to monkeys, habitually hold their bodies upright as they cling to a tree-trunk, sit on a bough, or arm-hang from a branch. And the typical primate limbs are long, with flexible joints for reaching.

One of the principal adaptations to two-legged walking is the change in the position of the foramen magnum. This is the opening through which the spinal cord enters the skull. In humans it is situated at the base of the skull, with the main muscle attachments on the lower surfaces of the skull bones. In apes this hole faces more towards the rear; ridges on the skull and spines on the neck vertebrae anchor the muscles that keep the head looking forwards.

In a bipedal animal the backbone (vertebral column) is designed to support weight from above and at the front, whereas in quadrupeds the horizontal girder-like back bone has the main body organs suspended below it. Seen from the side, it has an S-shaped shallow curve, marked in the lower back (lumbar region). The pelvis also adapts to bipedalism, being short, straight, and narrow. This brings the backbone more vertically above the legs. In apes the pelvis is longer and more curved when viewed from the side, so that the backbone leans forwards. Seen from the front, the human pelvis is broad, both to give side-to-side stability and encompass a wide birth canal for the large-brained infant. The bipedal femur is relatively long-necked and long-shafted, with less sideways curvature.

Able to straighten fully, the knee is adapted to withstand stresses in an upright position. The slight inwards angle brings the foot directly under the body, for economy of movement. The ankle is large, strong and firmly jointed.

The balance and forward propulsion required for a bipedal gait is enhanced by relatively short big toes which lie alongside the other toes. In apes the thumb-like big toe projects at an angle.

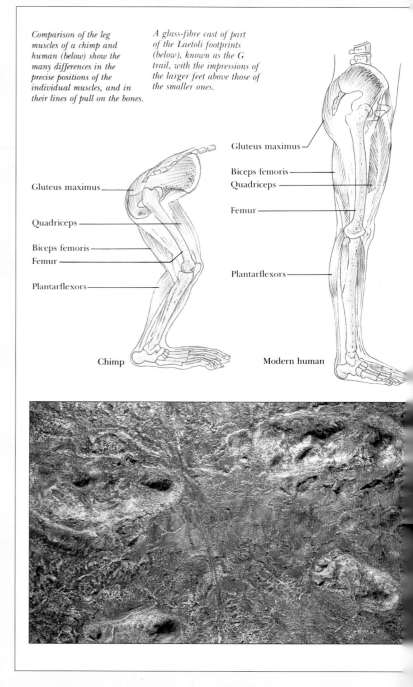

Comparison of the leg muscles of a chimp and human (below) show the many differences in the precise positions of the individual muscles, and in their lines of pull on the bones.

A glass-fibre cast of part of the Laetoli footprints (below), known as the G trail, with the impressions of the larger feet above those of the smaller ones.

Gluteus maximus

Quadriceps

Biceps femoris

Femur

Plantarflexors

Chimp

Gluteus maximus

Biceps femoris

Quadriceps

Femur

Plantarflexors

Modern human

The presence of these bipedal adaptations in a fossil skeleton provides major clues to dating and identification.

In the upright-walking human, the vertebral column or backbone in the neck joins the skull from almost directly below (far right). In the all-fours chimp, the vertebral column joins at an angle, partly from behind (right). At the site of the joint there is a large hole in the skull, the foramen magnum, through which the spinal cord joins the brain. Even on an isolated skull, therefore, the position of the foramen magnum is a clue to posture.

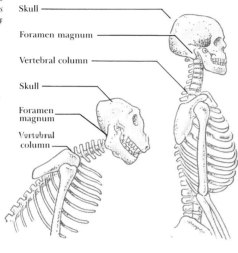

Skull

Foramen magnum

Vertebral column

Skull

Foramen magnum

Vertebral column

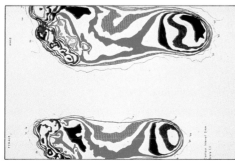

Modern footprints (left) in damp beach sand produce much the same impressions as those left by the australopithecines in the damp volcanic ash of Laetoli (far left). Photogrammetry shows depth as a series of coloured contour areas, the darkest colours indicating the deepest parts. The photogrammetric result of a modern human print (below left) shows weight distribution when walking, being greatest on the toes, ball and heel of the foot. It is very similar to that of the Laetoli prints.

The main Laetoli hominid trail is carefully cleaned (right). The prints of the two main individuals can be seen walking away from us. Notice how close their tracks are.

The not-so-glamorous stage of the search for our origins (above). The hot, dry, dusty conditions of East Africa are well conveyed by this photograph of field work at Koobi Fora. Surveying instruments, such as theodolites, are used to measure and map the site. The position of each fossil find is painstakingly recorded by notes, measurements, sketches, and photographs.

Australopithecus africanus. They are called *Australopithecus robustus*, the "robust southern ape," or *Paranthropus robustus*, the name used by Broom in the late 1930s.

In South Africa these creatures probably lived around 2–1.5 million years ago. The males stood 60 inches(1.5 metres) tall and weighed 130 pounds (60 kilos); the females were slightly smaller, possibly 90 pounds (40 kilos) in weight. The fossil bones have generous muscle-anchorage surfaces, indicating these animals had a powerful physique.

The skull, particularly in the male, shows gorilla-like bony ridges for attachment of the massive chewing muscles. The brain size is similar to a gorilla, too, at around 500 milliliters. But in contrast to the gorilla, the typical robust australopithecine had a broad, flat face, less projecting jaws, and a human-like skull base with the fora-men magnum towards the bottom, not the rear. The massive cheek teeth, tooth wear patterns, and strong jaw muscles all point to a diet of tough, hard-to-chew plant food.

THE EAST AFRICAN HOMINIDS: HOW MANY SPECIES?

The identification of australopithecines in East Africa is more complex than in the south. It is also interwoven with identifying other early hominids, such as those from our own genus *Homo*.

Towards the gracile end of the spectrum is *Australopithecus afarensis* already mentioned, as represented by Lucy and her kin. Fossil specimens of this group have been recovered from Hadar in Ethiopia and Laetoli in Tanzania. Some authorities say that many *Australopithecus afarensis* fossils are too similar to *Australopithecus africanus*, and the two were really the same species – or at least they exhibited "intergrading." The main age range for these fossils is about 3.5–3 million years. A jaw fragment from Baringo, Kenya, may also be from an individual of this type. It could be the earliest hominid fossil yet discovered, although its identification and dating remain debatable.

The *afarensis*-type creatures were fairly apelike, except for their well-developed upright walking already described. Their jaws protruded and carried big molars with a thick enamel covering, premolars which showed both ape and human characteristics, and smaller canines. Under the microscope, tooth wear patterns suggest a mainly vegetarian diet of fruit and leaves, perhaps with some meat.

In fact, at least two types of individuals are in these fossil collections. Some, like certain members of the "First Family," were large individuals with bony skull ridges, up to 60 inches (1.5 metres) and 155 pounds (70 kilos) in weight. Others, such as Lucy, were much smaller.

One interpretation is that these are males and females of the same species, *Australopithecus afarensis* (or *Australopithecus africanus*), and the differences are due to sexual dimorphism. The mainly ground-dwelling males could have been larger because they defended the group against predators, gathered or hunted food, and competed with each other for females – making large size an advantage. The smaller females may have spent some time in trees, especially with young offspring, rest-

ing and feeding. This is how gorillas live today. However the differences between the so-called male and female *Australopithecus afarensis* are even greater than for gorillas, themselves the most sexually dimorphic of living apes.

Another interpretation is that the fossils represent two or more species, and possibly not other australopithecines, either. The *afarensis*-type individuals could be assigned to *Australopithecus africanus*, while others could be early members of the genus *Homo* (page 72).

THE EAST AFRICAN ROBUSTS

As in South Africa, there are fossils from East Africa such as "Zinj" that suggest much bigger, more heavily built creatures than the gracile australopithecines. Over the years they have been variously classified: as the *Australopithecus robustus/Paranthropus robustus* species from South Africa, or as a separate group,

continued on page 66

In contrast to Koobi Fora (opposite), work in the shady parts of the South African caves such as at Makapansgat (below) is sometimes cool, even pleasant. But at other times the air is hot and stifling, with spotlights, sharp rocks and cramped conditions adding to the discomfort. Unpredictable rockfalls from the roof are an additional hazard.

A WALK IN EAST AFRICA

Australopithecine fossils give many clues to these hominids' size, posture, and ways of moving. But the areas of diet and lifestyle are more speculative. The African great apes (our closest living relatives) live in groups, and so do savannah-dwelling primates like baboons. So did the hominids that appeared later than the australopithecines, such as *Homo erectus*, and so do we. So it seems reasonable to assume creatures like *Australopithecus afarensis* were group-dwelling and had social systems of some kind. It is possible that, if the males were much larger than the females, this was the result of different roles within the group. The big males competed with each other for control of the group and mates, defended the group, and possibly hunted or scavenged meat. The smaller females cared for the young and perhaps gathered plants or smaller food items.

It is generally agreed that australopithecines stood and walked upright, though they may have stooped forwards slightly compared to humans of today. The trail of foot-prints from Laetoli has been called "dramatic and unassailable evidence" of their upright stance and bipedal gait. Recent evidence from the internal structure of the fossilised hip and leg bones also indicates that walking was their main way of moving about, although they may have climbed and used trees occasionally. Tooth structure and wear patterns suggest a diet of fruit, leaves, shoots, and other plant materials, with small amounts of meat. It is not clear whether the group members co-operated in food-finding, or whether they shared thier food with each other.

Could they talk? Almost all monkeys and apes communicate by facial gestures, body postures and sounds. It is likey the australopithecines did too. Natural rock casts showing the shape and contours of the brain (see Cranial endocasts, page 49) indicate that the parts of the brain concerned with speech were more developed in the australopithecines than in living apes. They may have used complex sets of sounds to communicate.

As the moon rises over a sleeping volcano in East Africa 3 million years ago, a group of gracile australopithecines makes its way through the darkening landscape, after a food-gathering trip. They carry sticks which they may have used as crude clubs or digging implements. Ever curious, like other apes and humans, one of them picks up a sick lizard and examines it as a potential meal.

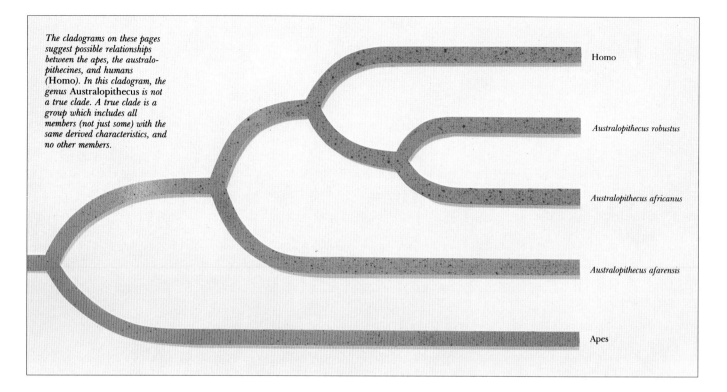

The cladograms on these pages suggest possible relationships between the apes, the australopithecines, and humans (Homo). In this cladogram, the genus Australopithecus is not a true clade. A true clade is a group which includes all members (not just some) with the same derived characteristics, and no other members.

Homo

Australopithecus robustus

Australopithecus africanus

Australopithecus afarensis

Apes

Australopithecus boisei (or even *Paranthropus boisei*). They lived about 2.5–1 million years ago, and their fossils are contemporary and from the same areas as other hominids, *Homo habilis* and *Homo erectus* (Chapters Four and Five). This indicates that several kinds of hominids coexisted about 1.5 million years ago.

The probable adaptations to a tough vegetarian diet are even more extreme in some of the East African robusts than in those from South Africa. The ridges and "crest" on the skull bone are further developed, the face almost concave, the cheekbones broad and "flaring," and the huge back teeth in even greater contrast to the tiny ones at the front. Like the other australopithecines, their brains are at or just above the brain-to-body ratios of today's apes.

THE ANCESTORS OF HUMANS?

To summarise, fossils indicate that several groups of australopithecine hominids lived in Africa, from about 4-1 million years ago. Were any of them our ancestors? This means looking at the age of the fossils, and possible relationships between the creatures they represent.

In this cladogram, the genus *Australopithecus* is a true clade. (This is indicated by the green colour.)

Assuming that hominid fossils of greater age will not be found elsewhere, it seems that Africa was the "home

of the hominids," or even the "birthplace of mankind." The earliest known hominids, from the Laetoli and Hadar regions 4–3 million years ago, seem to have evolved upright walking and human-like teeth, while much of their bodies, including their brains, were still relatively ape-like. One possibility is that they, in the form of *Australopithecus afarensis* or *africanus*, were ancestral to the other groups of australopithecines. One evolutionary line led via *africanus* to the robust-type australopithecines. The other led to *Homo*. There are various other shufflings of the groups, as shown in the cladograms.

It is generally agreed that the robust australopithecines were something of an evolutionary dead end. They left no fossils younger than 1 million years, and no more recent creatures are linked to them. Yet a further possibility is that another, still undiscovered group from 5 million or more years ago were ancestors of both the australopithecines and our own genus, *Homo*. Crucial to this question is the identification and age of the oldest *Homo* fossils. As mentioned above, some scientists identify the Hadar/Laetoli remains as being *afarensis*, with *Homo* fossils preserved only in later rocks, thereby giving enough time for the former to evolve into the latter. Others say that early *Homo* is represented at about the same time as afarensis (or rather *africanus*), in which case the latter cannot be the ancestor of the former.

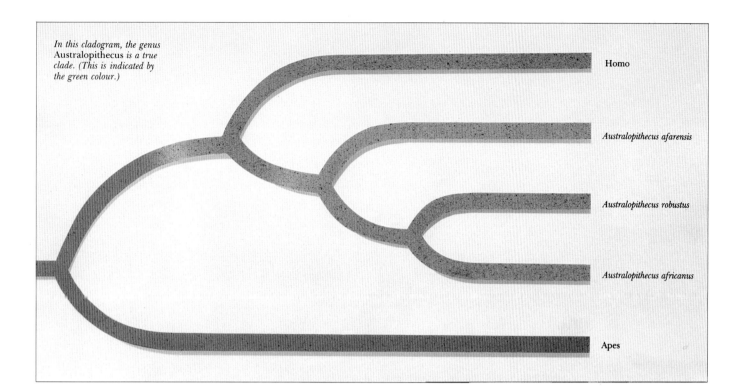

In this cladogram, the genus Australopithecus *is a true clade. (This is indicated by the green colour.)*

Homo

Australopithecus afarensis

Australopithecus robustus

Australopithecus africanus

Apes

In 1978, Donald Johanson wrote to Mary Leakey concerning the naming of Lucy and her fellows: "Why not *Homo*? The Laetoli/Hadar material does not show the hall-mark of the genus *Homo*...the brain is still small and has not yet commenced enlargement." Having taken to upright walking in the early phase of hominid evolution, the search for the enlarging brain is the next great step.

THE
FIRST
HUMANS

On April 4, 1964, the palaeontologist-cum-explorer Louis Leakey, with anatomist colleagues Phillip Tobias of the University of Witwatersrand, Johannesburg, and John Napier of London University, announced the discovery of a new kind of human. Their report in the science journal *Nature* described fossils dated at about 1.7 million years old, of what they claimed was the earliest known human. They named its kind *Homo habilis*. *Homo* means "human" or "man." The second part of the name translates approximately as "able, competent, handy, mentally skilled." Thus *Homo habilis*, alleged maker of the first tools, soon assumed the appropriate nickname of "Handy Man."

The reaction to the announcement was, to say the least, mixed. Various experts disagreed with the interpretation of the fossils, with the reconstruction of the creature they represented, with the reasons for placing them in the genus *Homo*, and even with the name chosen. Today, the credibility of *Homo habilis* as a distinct species, and its standing as a grade of humanity, are still the subject of argument.

THE SHORT REIGN OF ZINJ

Louis Leakey had previously attempted to announce the discovery of one of our ancestors. This was with the extremely robust australopithecine "Zinj" (Chapter Three), a fossil skull found at Olduvai in 1959. At first he regarded Zinj and his kind as sufficiently different from the robust australopithecines of South Africa, and sufficiently similar to ourselves, to merit their inclusion in the genus *Homo*.

This interpretation was reinforced by the numerous stone tools scattered around the site where Zinj lay, along with the broken bones of many animals, on what seemed to be some sort of flattened living floor. Since Zinj's skull did not show signs of being split or damaged by "an animal agency" before it fossilized, the assumption was that he was the maker of the stone tools and thus, despite his small brain, an early human. In 1960 Leakey wrote: "It is precisely by his manufacture of the first known pattern of implements that I believe *Zinjanthropus* can claim the title of earliest man at least until other, more distant toolmakers are found."

Only a few months later, Leakey's team began to find the "jumble of fossils" which they eventually used to establish *Homo habilis*.

A "JUMBLE OF FOSSILS"

The first of these fossils were two lower-leg bones, some yards from each other and the Zinj skull. They were of lighter build than most robust australopithecine bones.

Wildebeest and zebra migrate across the modern-day Tanzanian plains, in search of fresh pasture. The scene has probably been repeated countless times over the millennia. Early humans may have hunted or scavenged the large grazing herds of their time, 1–2 million years ago.

Next Jonathan Leakey, eldest son of Louis and Mary, found some hominid fragments at a site nearby in mid-1960. Gradually more bits came to light: teeth, finger and foot bones, a collarbone, braincase fragments, and a lower jaw, scattered over an area of several square yards. Some of these were identified as belonging to a juvenile individual about 12 years old. But it was not a heavily built, small-brained, robust type of hominid. The bones were thinner and lighter, and the curvature of the braincase fragments suggested that they contained a larger brain. The fossils were found in very slightly older layers than Zinj, and were known informally for a time as the "pre-Zinj child".

Over the following months and years further pieces were found: a partial upper braincase, a lower jaw with 13 teeth, and other pieces including bits of rib, hand, and foot. Leakey reported each find in the scientific press, but did not speculate in public about the creature they came from. The anatomist John Napier studied the hand bones and agreed that the thumb could "oppose" the fingers (touch each of their tips in turn), giving the precision grip thought necessary for making the tools at the site. Another anatomist, Michael Day, studied the foot bones and reassembled a humanlike foot, lacking the divergent big toe of the apes, and capable of an upright, striding gait. Privately, Leakey kept in touch with a leading British palaeoanthropologist, Wilfred Le Gros Clark in Oxford. Le Gros Clark and several other colleagues thought the fossils were probably from an australopithecine, but Leakey was not deterred.

As often happens, part of the problem was not connected with the fossils themselves, but how they were viewed within the prevailing scientific opinions of the day. This newly discovered creature would have lived alongside the robust *boisei*-type australopithecines, as evidenced by Zinj. The idea of two hominids living "side by side" was almost unheard of at the time. (Thirty years later, suggestions that perhaps up to five hominid species lived at about the same time in East Africa raise few eyebrows.)

HOMO HABILIS TAKES THE STAGE

Another difficulty was that naming a new species in an existing genus requires careful explanation: how is it similar to other species in the genus, and how does it dif-

The FLK excavation site at Olduvai Gorge (below). Louis Leakey found the first stone tools here in 1931. The site was named in honor of his first wife Frida Leakey (FL), followed by Korongo, the Swahili word for gulley. At the same site, Mary Leakey discovered "Zinj" in 1959. Further work showed FLK was a living floor used by hominids who made Oldowan tools – presumably Homo habilis.

Phillip Tobias, one of the authors of the 1964 scientific paper which announced the discovery of a new fossil hominid species, Homo habilis. *His estimate of its cranial capacity at 680 millilitres (24 floz) set it apart from the australopithecines. Here he is seen lecturing at Sterkfontein, South Africa.*

fer from other members in closely related genera? Why *Homo habilis*, not *Australopithecus habilis*?

One of the main criteria for being *Homo* was brain size. Different authorities had different threshold sizes, ranging from 700-800 millilitres (25-28 floz). Most australopithecines were around 500 millilitres (18 floz), while *Homo erectus* (Chapter Five) was above 1,000 millilitres (36 floz). What of the new discovery?

In their announcement Leakey, Tobias, and Napier proposed that a brain size of more than 600 millilitres (21 floz) would suffice for inclusion in *Homo*, along with other features indicated by the fossils, such as upright posture and two-legged walking, and a precision grip in the hand. It happened that this first *Homo habilis* specimen had a brain size estimated at 680 millilitres (24 floz).

Other *habilis*-type fossils were being discovered at Olduvai Gorge. In three places they were associated with the simple stone tools already known for decades, and called the Oldowan stone-tool culture (after the gorge). Was this further support for creation of a new species?

This suggestion generated more lively debate. It was centered around tool-making. Tools have been called "frozen behaviour," and proposals about their manufacture and use have many behavioral and cultural implications. But they are not actual fossils of the crea-

tures themselves. Classification has always been established solely on the physical attributes of the fossilised remains of animals or plants, and their morphology. Many authorities were unhappy about tools as admissible evidence in support of this new species.

The naming of *Homo habilis* also sparked off yet another "splitters versus lumpers" debate. Some biologists and palaeontologists tend to minimise the number of groups they are dealing with. If a new fossil form is discovered, they try hard to place it in one of the existing categories. Only if compelled by exceptional and unique features, do they approve of establishing a new taxon (a taxonomic group, ranging from a sub-species to a phylum). They are "lumpers." The "splitters," on the other hand, tend to create new groups – taxonomic subspecies, species, genera, even families – much more easily. The history of hominid fossil discoveries, in particular, is littered with names coined in the excitement of a new find. Many of these names have not stood the test of time.

A TRANSITIONAL FORM?

In the mid-1960s, many people (but not Leakey) thought it probable that *Homo erectus* had evolved from some type of australopithecine. Therefore, the lumpers argued, it would be natural to find fossils rep-

A portrait of skull 1470, reconstructed from the hundreds of fragments painstakingly gathered from the Koobi Fora site. The larger intact pieces at the top gave early clues to this hominid's relatively large, rounded cranium (braincase), compared with those of the australopithecines.

transitional form and wrote of the fossils: "What we did not suppose was that the discoverer would create a new species to contain them." Le Gros Clark added, on the basis of the early samples of this taxonomic group, that "Homo habilis" (his quotation marks) was "easily accommodated within *Australopithecus africanus*," and hoped that the new species would disappear as rapidly as it came – a hope that was not realised.

There were plenty of other opinions about where *Homo habilis* fitted into the hominid evolutionary tree. Leakey himself long held the view that our modern species *Homo sapiens* was in fact very ancient, and could be a direct descendant of *Homo habilis*. This would push *Homo erectus* out onto a limb, making it our cousin and not our ancestor. He always hoped that fossils would show that tool-making humans were alive perhaps 7 million years ago. This would push the australopithecines out on a limb, too, making them a parallel genus to the human one, and making it impossible for any known australopithecine group to be ancestral to humans.

The pendulum of opinion has swung to and fro since *Homo habilis* hit the headlines. Some authorities call the creature "habilines," in a similar way to the use of the term "australopithecines." This is a convenient shorthand way of acknowledging that the fossils represent some kind of grade, but without according them full status as a separate taxonomic rank. Another term is the somewhat vaguer "early *Homo*."

SKULL 1470

One of the most important hominid fossils, and after much argument now generally accepted as habiline, was discovered by Louis Leakey's son, Richard. He established field camps in the Koobi Fora area of East Turkana, in Kenya, in the late 1960s. In 1969 the fossil skull of a robust australopithecine was recovered there. Another, more fragmented skull codenamed 407 aroused great excitement at the time, due to its apparent combination of *Homo* and gracile australopithecine features. But this was eventually identified as probably a female skull of the *boisei*-type australopithecine group.

On 27 August, 1972 at Koobi Fora, team member Bernard Ngeneo spotted a few promising fossil scraps being exposed and eroded from sandstone in a steep gulley. Eventually some 300 fragments of skull were carefully picked from the rocky, arid site. The curvature of

resenting an in-between "transitional form" – the result of evolution in action. Rather than create a separate species, this new form should be placed either with its predecessors, the australopithecines, or (much less likely) with its successor, *Homo erectus*. The splitters argued that the fossils were sufficiently different from any of the australopithecines, and certainly from *Homo erectus*, to merit their own species.

In fact, Louis Leakey had a reputation as a "supersplitter." He had already created numerous new species and genera of ancient hominids, most of which became subsumed into other groups. Would *Homo habilis* be another example? The anthropologist Bernard Campbell from Cambridge, England, regarded it as a

Richard Leakey pauses thoughtfully at area 131, Koobi Fora (above). The marker at the bottom identifies the area of skull 1470.

AGE CONCERN: THE KBS TUFF

Skull 1470 suffered from a dating problem that highly coloured its initial interpretations. The drama unfolded as follows:

● *Graduate paleontologist Kay Behrensmeyer discovered some Oldowan-type pebble tools at Koobi Fora in 1969, the first full season of excavations there. They were embedded in a whitish-grey layer of hardened volcanic ash, or tuff, which became known at the camp as the KBS-Kay Behrensmeyer Site.*

● *Since the rock in the KBS layer was volcanic, this offered the possibility of potassium-argon radiodating. Samples were taken and sent to Cambridge, England. They were initially dated by the geophysicist Jack Miller at 200 million years old! This enormous age was assumed to be caused by contamination by older rocks, perhaps during erosion by a stream.*

● *New rock samples, of feldspar crystals, were sent from Koobi Fora and dated by Miller and colleague Frank Fitch at 2.4 million years old, revised to 2.6 million. The KBS dates were used as a standard for other rocks and fossils from the area.*

● *Three years later, skull 1470 came from rocks below the KBS tuff. This implied it was older than the tuff – maybe nearly 3 million years old. If true, then the origins of* Homo *were pushed right back by these dates.*

● *But problems with this great age soon surfaced. Fossils of other animals at Koobi Fora, dated relative to the KBS tuff, did not seem to fit into the general scheme for East Africa.*

● *In particular, the sequence of Koobi Fora pig fossils seemed to occur at least half a million years earlier than a very similar sequence of pig fossils from Omo, 90 miles away. Omo was becoming famous for the excellent series of animal fossils and volcanic rocks which allowed thorough dating.*

● *In 1974, another laboratory dated the relevant samples from Koobi Fora at 1.8 million years old. But fission-track dating confirmed the 2.6 million years age.*

● *Eventually it was agreed: there had been a mix-up. It was not clear whether the rock samples were collected from other places, or contaminated, or whether the early potassium-argon technique used was unreliable. But 1470 relinquished its claim as the "World's Oldest Man." It was redated at about 1.8 million years old, almost the same as the original* Homo habilis *specimens from Olduvai Gorge.*

two of the larger intact pieces, from the upper forehead/temple area, indicated it was a relatively large-brained hominid. The skull's initial reconstruction by Meave Leakey (Richard"s wife) and anatomist Bernard Wood fulfilled this promise. The skull was logged as KNM-ER 1470 (Kenya National Museum, East Rudolf). It has since been known to the world as "1470".

Skull 1470 came from a rock layer just below an outcrop of volcanic tuff – ash from a nearby volcano which had been compressed and chemically cemented into stone. This particular outcrop, known as the KBS tuff, was significant at the Koobi Fora site because it had been radiodated a few years previously, at 2.6 million years old.

What did 1470 represent? It had some australopithecine characteristics, a face flattened from side to side but projecting forwards to a degree. Exactly which degree depended, since the face seemed to fit the braincase at several angles. The upper jaw was relatively large, and held sizeable teeth comparable to those of modern humans. But the major feature was the high forehead and bulging, thin-boned braincase. Early estimates of brain size were 800 millilitres (28 floz) A brain of this size surely meant the creature should be a member of the genus *Homo*?

Some experts ventured that it was a peculiarly large-brained australopithecine. Richard Leakey himself doubted this. He also doubted at first that it was *Homo habilis*, since its brain was more than 100 millilitres (3.5 floz) larger, and its age almost 1 million years older, than the typical *habilis* specimens from Olduvai Gorge. When the remarkable fossil was described in the scientific press, Richard Leakey was mindful of the storm over his father's announcement of *Homo habilis* 20 years earlier. He proposed that it be referred to as *Homo* sp. indet. (species indeterminate). Therefore it was human, and the oldest human fossil so far discovered, by almost 1 million years. 1470 soon became "The World's Oldest Man." Its great age was used to throw doubt on the suggestion that *Homo* had evolved from an australopithecine ancestor, since it was older than many australopithecine fossils, too.

It was conjectured that the skull of "1470 Man" had become fossilised after being covered by silt, from the waters of Lake Turkana. The lake had changed size and shape through ancient times. Today, 1470 is regarded by some authorities as a fine example of *Homo habilis*. Because of problems with the KBS tuff dating, the fossil now has the revised age of 1.8 million years.

OTHER KOOBI FORA CONTENDERS

Several other skulls have been discovered at Koobi Fora, which only seem to complicate the picture. Number 1813 has *habilis*-like teeth and a generally flatter, human-type face, unlike the australopithecines, but its brain is much smaller, around 510 millilitres (18 floz). It is estimated to be 1.7-1.5 million years old, and suggestions of its identity range from a variant of *Australopithecus africanus* to an early, and possibly new species of *Homo*. Another skull has quite human-looking teeth but a small brain 580 millilitres (20 floz) and bony ridges or crests, like the robust australopithecines. Again, it has not been positively identified.

THE HABILINE PROFILE

More than 20 *Homo habilis* individuals have been found at Olduvai since the pioneering work in the 1960s. The South African sites of Swartkrans and Sterkfontein have also yielded *habilis*-like specimens, as well as Omo. From the assembled fossil evidence, it is thought that habilines lived in East Africa around

KOOBI FORA

The Koobi Fora peninsula is on the eastern side of Lake Turkana (formerly Lake Rudolf) in northern Kenya. Its fossil potential was noticed by Richard Leakey as he flew over the area in 1967. Fossil-containing sandstone sediments alternate with volcanic ash falls which can be radiodated. Since work began there in the late 1960s, Koobi Fora has yielded many important hominid fossils, including those attributed to the boisei-type robust australopithecines, Homo habilis or other forms of early Homo, as well as the earliest Homo erectus remains.

2.3–1.6 million years ago. Typical *habilis* members (if there are such creatures, as discussed later) were about 1.3 metres (50 inches) tall, and probably weighed around 40 kilos (90 pounds). Many aspects of their skeletal remains, from the backbones through the hips, to the legs and feet, show that they habitually stood and walked upright, although some studies propose that they were also "handy" at climbing and moving around in trees. Hand reconstructions endow them with both the precision and power grips (page 96).

Comparisons with australopithecines show at once the skull"s much more rounded eyebrow ridges, with a more vertical forehead and bulging braincase, giving a brain volume of 700-800 millilitres (25-28 floz). The face is flatter but still projecting, not almost vertical as in modern humans. The slimmer jaws bear smaller, more humanlike teeth, especially the canines. The tooth wear patterns indicate an omnivore: both plants and meat were in the diet.

Besides having a bigger brain than australopithecines

or living apes, *Homo habilis* also had a higher brain-to-body ratio. Compared to apes, the temporal lobes which deal with memory and other mental functions are more developed; so are the parietal lobes, which analyse information coming in from the senses; while the speech-processing Broca's area, absent in apes, is also developed. The occipital lobes, which deal with information from the eyes, are smaller. Brain development can also be assessed indirectly by the behavioural achievements of *Homo habilis*. The central feature here is making and using tools.

TOOLS OF THE TRADE

The simple types of stone tools assumed to be the work of *Homo habilis*, called Oldowan, have also been found at numerous other sites, sometimes associated with *habilis* fossils, sometimes with the fossilised bones of other animals, and sometimes alone. (It is likely, but not certain, that the habilines were the only toolmakers.)

The earliest Oldowan tools are 2.5 million years old, from Hadar in Ethiopia. The types of stones used were often not naturally present at the sites where they were found, showing that these hominids fashioned raw materials they had collected elsewhere. In some cases the nearest "tool quarry" was 12 miles away.

Excavations at Omo. Each working site is divided into a grid of squares with strings, wires, or strips of wood. The loose material is brushed away and the rocks are carefully examined for fossils. Each square is then slowly removed, piece by piece, to a predetermined depth. Many sketches, maps, and photographs record the progress

OLDUVAI GORGE

The eastern 12 miles of Olduvai Gorge in northern Tanzania. Half of this huge scar across the landscape is a fossil gold-mine:

• layers of sediments contain literally thousands upon thousands of fossils of all manner of creatures, from shrews to extinct relatives of elephants. Studies have shown how the climate and environment changed through the ages.

• the fossil-bearing strata alternate with layers of volcanic rock. Nearby volcanoes erupted intermittently, showering the vicinity and preserving the animal and plant matter. These volcanic beds can be accurately dated, so supplying a reliable timescale for the fossils between them.

• the lowest layers at Olduvai are almost 2 million years old. Their fossils can be used as

benchmarks to allow relative dating of the fossil-bearing layers from other sites, which contain similar remains.

• many fossils are undisturbed, lying exactly as they were when the volcanic shower covered them. The relative positions of bones and stone tools permit many conclusions about the tool-makers and their ancient campsites.

• depthwise, the site has been occupied by various hominids and other animals, more often than not, for close to 2 million years. Lengthwise, more than 120 study sites are scattered along the gorge. Thus Olduvai provides an astonishingly complete cross-section of human and prehuman history.

THE OLDUVAI TOOLKIT

These are some of the Oldowan-type tools found at various African sites:

● *choppers*, one of the main tool types. They fit into the hand and can be wielded with power, as an all-purpose item for smashing bones or hard plant foods like nuts.

● *sharp stone flakes* for cutting and slicing. These are held naturally between the thumb and fingers, in a precision grip. They could have been for slitting skin, slicing tendons (sinews), or cutting open fruits and stems to get at the soft flesh within.

● *scrapers*, sharpened along one edge and held in a power grip. They were possibly for scraping skin, or meat from bones.
● *hammer-stones*, for striking other rocks and making them into tools.

Rounded quartz pebble tool, 1–2 million years old

Handaxe shaped from a lava pebble, 1.4 million years old

The DK stone circle at Olduvai (below), sheltered and protected from further erosion. It has been suggested that the deliberately placed stones represent the outline of an early hut-like dwelling. Another interpretation is that the pattern was created by the roots of a large tree!

There are two main categories of tools.

Core tools These are modified pebbles, mostly selected so that they fit nicely in the hand using the power grip. They range from the "size of a pingpong ball to that of a croquet ball," as described by Louis Leakey. Several flakes were struck off the core, usually using a hammer-stone, to give a sharp edge along its side or around its end.

Flake tools These are the flakes struck from the core. They are held best with the precision grip, and are generally thinner and more bladelike.

Thousands of tools recovered from numerous sites at Olduvai Gorge trace gradual developments in their manufacture. In Bed I, the lowest level excavated and almost 2 million years old, there are about six main tool types. By about 1 million years ago, in Bed II, this number has risen to ten, and the tools themselves are marginally more sophisticated, known as Developed Oldowan.

What were the tools for? An immediate assumption is that they were for catching, killing, and butchering animals, for food. The tool evolution is reflected in the bones of the victims. In the younger layers there are fewer fossilised bones, but they are from bigger animals such as elephants, rhinos, hippos, and giraffes. Perhaps the extra effort in catching a big victim was worth it, for

the large amount of extra food obtained.

What were they made of? Flint, the stone favoured by European Stone Age people, does not occur in the area. Tools in Beds I and II were mainly shaped from blocks of solidified lava, generally collected from about a mile away. In Bed III, rocks have been carried up to 6 miles. (Whether the tools were made at the collection site, or carried back to the living site and then manufactured, is not clear.) Chert was also employed. By Bed IV, the tool-makers were using various rocks such as gneiss, trachyte and phonolite, from sources up to 13 miles away. Developed Oldowan tools made from different rocks were not discovered in clumps, close to their source, but they seem to crop up at random all over the area.

This mass of evidence suggests several conclusions. There are advancing mental abilities involved in planning to make a tool, selecting a certain type and shape of stone for it, and physically shaping it with careful manipulative control. There is also the design factor, choosing the best type of tool for the job. From the fairly random distribution of the different rock types, it seems likely that groups of toolmakers may have shared or exchanged stone.

FOOD-SHARING?

Some tools were found at "kill sites." They are often associated with fossil animal bones, and they could simply have been made on the spot, used as disposable instruments to cut up the carcass, and then abandoned as the makers moved on.

The fact that there were tools suited to butchering meat, and bones of animals far too big for one or a few hominids to eat, suggests a picture of hunting groups bringing down large prey, and sharing the food among themselves and possibly with others.

Marks on the fossil animal bones could have been made by the stone cutting tools. But research and observation have shown that similar marks can be produced in a number of ways, such as the bones being trampled by passing creatures! The evidence for the exact way tools were used is equivocal.

CAMP SITES AND LIVING FLOORS

Olduvai provides excellent evidence of "sites of hominid activity or occupation," where the ground is littered with tools, bones, horns and other objects, and sometimes flattened – presumably by tramping feet. These places are also called living floors, activity areas or simply camp sites.

The oldest were in use 1.9 million years ago. There are up to 20 sites in Bed I, and most would have been situated near permanent water, on the ancient lake edge, near where streams flowed in. The lake waxed and waned through prehistory, but by Bed II it has almost disappeared. The 60-plus sites so far located in these layers, and the 40-plus in Beds III and IV, are generally near pools, small lakes or watercourses of some kind. Indeed, the pattern of occupation sites traces the changing drainage of the area over the millennia. From the bottom of Bed I to the top of Bed II, a time span of 700,000 million years, there are more than 40 levels of hominid occupation.

Many of these sites have tools lying about, and animal bones smashed and broken before fossilisation. Sometimes the site seems to have been abandoned just

continued on page 80

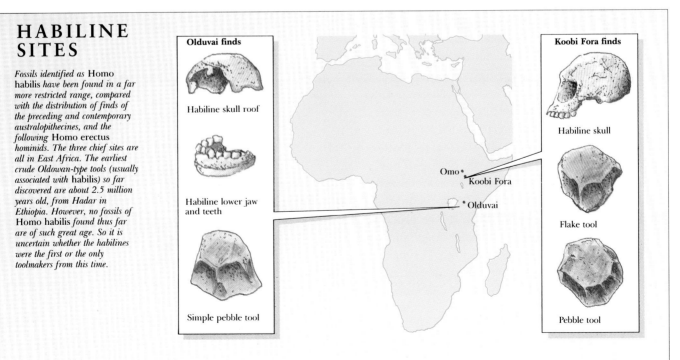

HABILINE SITES

Fossils identified as Homo habilis *have been found in a far more restricted range, compared with the distribution of finds of the preceding and contemporary australopithecines, and the following* Homo erectus *hominids. The three chief sites are all in East Africa. The earliest crude Oldowan-type tools (usually associated with* habilis*) so far discovered are about 2.5 million years old, from Hadar in Ethiopia. However, no fossils of* Homo habilis *found thus far are of such great age. So it is uncertain whether the habilines were the first or the only toolmakers from this time.*

Olduvai finds

Habiline skull roof

Habiline lower jaw and teeth

Simple pebble tool

Omo
Koobi Fora
Olduvai

Koobi Fora finds

Habiline skull

Flake tool

Pebble tool

LIFE ON THE LAKESHORE

From the assembled evidence, how did the habilines spend their days in East Africa, close to 2 million years ago? Like other humans and also the closely related apes, they probably lived in groups. Evidence of living floors and accumulations of tools, bones, and the general debris of living – particularly at Olduvai Gorge – suggests that habilines or other hominids settled for a time in one place, the "camp site," before moving on. On their travels they would gather plant foods and perhaps hunt or scavenge a variety of game, such as antelopes and gazelles.

Early stone tools, of the Oldowan tradition, are associated with habiline remains. Tools of wood, antler, and bone may have also been in use, but these have not been preserved. The hominids could have carried stone tools with them, in order to kill, skin, and cut up the catch. Or they might have quickly fashioned the tools from convenient nearby materials, when suitable game was sighted or caught. The habilines' litter of discarded tools and stones, broken bones, and other fragments is valuable circumstantial evidence for the view that they were the first of our ancestors to include meat as a major part of their diet.

Possibly the habiline people built simple hut-like shelters at some camp sites. Probably they spent time experimenting with various rocks and learning about different shapes of tools. They may have used pebbles as simple hammers to smash open fruits, bones, and other food items. Then they noticed, compared to their own hands and teeth, the sharp edge of a naturally chipped pebble could easily slice open hard-cased fruits to get at the soft flesh, or cut stringy meat and tendons from the bones of a scavenged victim. This meant more types and sources of food became available. Gradually, through the processes of observation, reasoning, and experimentation, they developed ways of using these tools. The next great advance was to make them – select a pebble, and hit it in the right way, to remove fragments and leave a sharp edge.

A mixed-age Homo habilis *family group "at home" outside their roughly constructed shelter. The lake in the background provides fresh water for drinking, and perhaps food in the form of water plants, fish, and other aquatic creatures. One adult member uses a crudely shaped* pebble tool to break open an animal bone, gaining access to the nutritious marrow within. The younger individual watches, copies, and learns.

HOMO HABILIS AND MODERN HUMANS

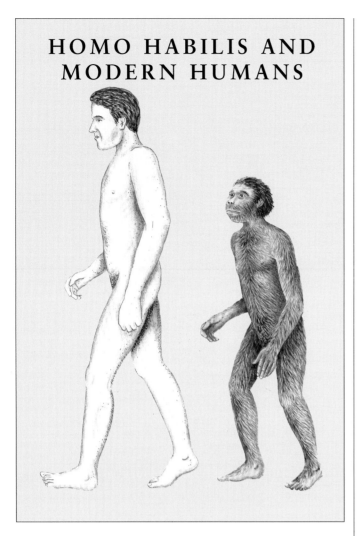

A typical representative of Homo habilis *would have been considerably shorter than the average modern European or North American. It would also have been smaller and less powerfully built than its contemporary, the robust boisei-type australopithecine. Body weight is estimated at about 88 pounds (40 kilograms). As in all such reconstructions the skin colour, and the colour, length, and distribution of the hair, are conjectural.*

before the shower of preserving volcanic ash, which blanketed the bones and stones and left them undisturbed from when the occupiers "downed tools." The floor where Zinj was found is one example. It is more than 83 sq. metres (300 square yards) in area, and contained more than 2,400 tools and other artifacts (the catch-all term for deliberately-made, non-natural items). There seem to be two chief piles of animal debris – one of marrow-containing bones, the other of bones which do not have marrow inside.

The first evidence of purpose-made shelter, even a simple building construction, may also come from Olduvai. At the site known as DK is a rough circle about 4 metres

(4 yards) across, of solidified lava blocks, up to 30 centimetres (12 inches) high. Could this be the foundation of a hut, maybe fashioned from branches, or the base of a windbreak screen? The site is on a small mound, and the fossil bones of flamingoes (which are lake birds) and bits of fish, along with what look like the roots of reeds, could indicate that this was a dry "island" in a marshy lakeshore.

ADDED COMPLEXITY

In 1986 at Olduvai Gorge, a partial fossilised skeleton known as OH 62 came to light. It is 1.8 million years old, and the bits of skull, jaws and limbs seem to be "in definite association" – they represent one individual. And a very small one: an adult female hominid, between 1-1.1 metres (40 and 44 inches) tall, with long arms and hands hanging at her knees. She seems to have had a habilis-like head, but a body more reminiscent of *Australopithecus afarensis*, with a few ape-like characteristics, too. Some skeletal features indicate she was adept at climbing and moving around in trees, as well as walking upright on two legs.

OH 62 and other recent discoveries from the main East African sites are being analysed, and attempts are under way to fit them into the pattern of hominid evolution. One opinion is that the large and small habiline-like fossils represent males and females of one species – *Homo habilis* itself. The size and other differences are examples of sexual dimorphism. There are also differences due to the usual individual variation within a group, and to the variation between groups from different locations.

Another opinion is that the differences are too marked for there to be a single, credible species. Skeletons attributed to the habiline group vary in height from just over 1-1.5 metres (40 inches to more than 60 inches); some of the bigger specimens have heavier faces and generally more australopithecinelike features. It has been calculated that the sexual dimorphism indicated by these so-called *habilis* remains exceeds that between the huge male and small female gorillas, themselves the most sexually dimorphic of our near relatives.

The creeping conclusion here is that the *habilis* net has been cast too wide. It is highly likely that at least some of the fossils must be of creatures from a different species (or even more than one). Should a new name be proposed to accommodate them? This is where *Homo*

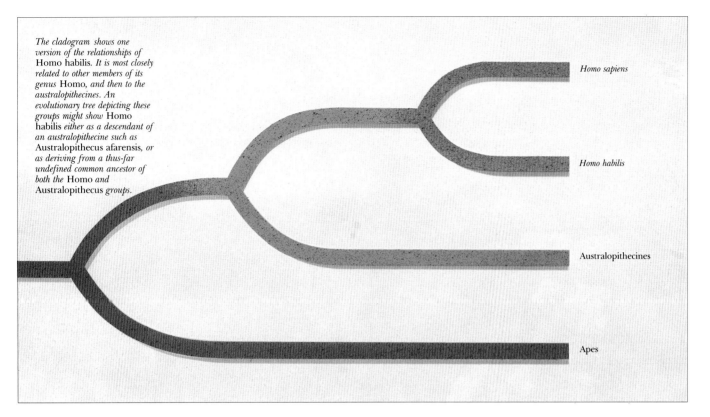

The cladogram shows one version of the relationships of Homo habilis. *It is most closely related to other members of its genus* Homo, *and then to the australopithecines. An evolutionary tree depicting these groups might show* Homo habilis *either as a descendant of an australopithecine such as* Australopithecus afarensis, *or as deriving from a thus-far undefined common ancestor of both the* Homo *and* Australopithecus *groups.*

Homo sapiens

Homo habilis

Australopithecines

Apes

habilis came in.

THE EVOLUTIONARY PERSPECTIVE

The version of our evolutionary tree in which *Australopithecus afarensis* gave rise to *Homo habilis*, which evolved into *Homo erectus*, which in turn produced *Homo sapiens*, has an appealingly neat straightline feel to it. But standing back from the main habilis time period, about 1.9–1.6 million years ago, brings various complications.

What about before the habilines? An alternative to the *afarensis-habilis-erectus-sapiens* view is that "early *Homo*" was already living at Hadar more than 3 million years ago. To allow for the diversity of australopithecines and other hominids in Africa around 3–2 million years ago, this *Homo* evolutionary line may have split from the other hominids 5 or more million years ago. Then, gradually, early *Homo* became *Homo sapiens*. Whether it passed through the *habilis* and/or *erectus* stages on the way, or whether one or both of these groups were not our ancestors but our cousins, on sidebranches of the tree, is another area of lively debate.

What about after the habilines? By 1.6 million years ago, another human species had appeared – the taller, long-legged, bigger-brained *Homo erectus*. If *habilis* did

evolve into *erectus*, could such a great evolutionary change have taken place so quickly? It is difficult to conceive of small hominids such as OH 62 developing into large hominids such as "West Turkana Boy," in 200,000 years or less. One possibility is a punctuation – a rapid burst of change in the type of evolutionary process known as punctuated equilibrium. Another is that some relatively isolated habiline population(s) began to evolve into *erectus* at a much earlier date, leaving the rest of their kind to continue unchanged, and eventually go extinct about 1.6 million years ago.

The time between 2 and 1.5 million years ago has been called the "crucial humanizing period." Recent fossil finds from this time have widened the debate as to how many species of hominids lived in Africa then, and who evolved into what. More fossils may serve either to clarify the picture, or further confuse it.

CHAPTER

HUMANS
SPREAD FROM
AFRICA

Java is a large island a few degrees south of the Equator, and home to the capital of the Republic of Indonesia, Jakarta. Before Indonesia gained independence in 1945, Java had been under the control of the Netherlands, as part of the Dutch East Indies, for almost 150 years. In the 1890s the island came to attention as the site where a Dutch scientist proclaimed he had found a missing link: "Java Man."

Eugene Dubois had been a keen fossil-hunter as a boy in the Netherlands. He studied medicine at the University of Amsterdam, and in 1886 he lectured there in anatomy. But he always hoped to travel and discover "fossil man," having been inspired by the writings of the famous naturalist Alfred Wallace and the German biologist Ernst Haeckel. It was Wallace who had co-proposed the theory of evolution by natural selection with Charles Darwin, and who had worked and collected specimens in the Malayan region for several years – and who had speculated that, because orangs and gibbons live in southeastern Asia, early humans may have once lived and evolved there.

A DUTCHMAN IN JAVA

In 1887 Dubois took his family to the Dutch East Indies as a military surgeon for the Dutch East India Army. At once he began his search for fossils, having retained his boyhood interests in geology and palaeontology. He worked first in Sumatra, then transferred to Java. During this time he supervised the collection of more than 12,000 fossils, of creatures ranging from fish to elephants and hippos, near Mount Lawu. But there were no apes or humans.

In 1890 the Dutch anatomist moved his attention to the banks of the Solo River, near the village of Trinil. At a bend in the river, layers of sandstone and volcanic ash had been exposed by erosion; it looked a likely site for fossils. In September 1891 the excavators came upon an interesting human-like fossil tooth. The next month they chanced to find a preserved partial skullcap. It was part of the "roof" of the skull, over the brain. It consisted of thick bone, with a low vault or curve that meant the brain beneath was perhaps only half as big as in a modern human. At the front of the skullcap, above the missing eyes, were prominent, projecting brow ridges.

At first Dubois thought the fossils were of a large, extinct type of chimp. The team continued to dig into the riverbank. The next year they uncovered a thigh bone. It came from a new location about 15 yards upstream from the tooth and skullcap, but in the same rock layers. In contrast to the ape-like skull, the thigh bone was remarkably similar to that of a modern human. It obviously came from a creature that walked upright, like us.

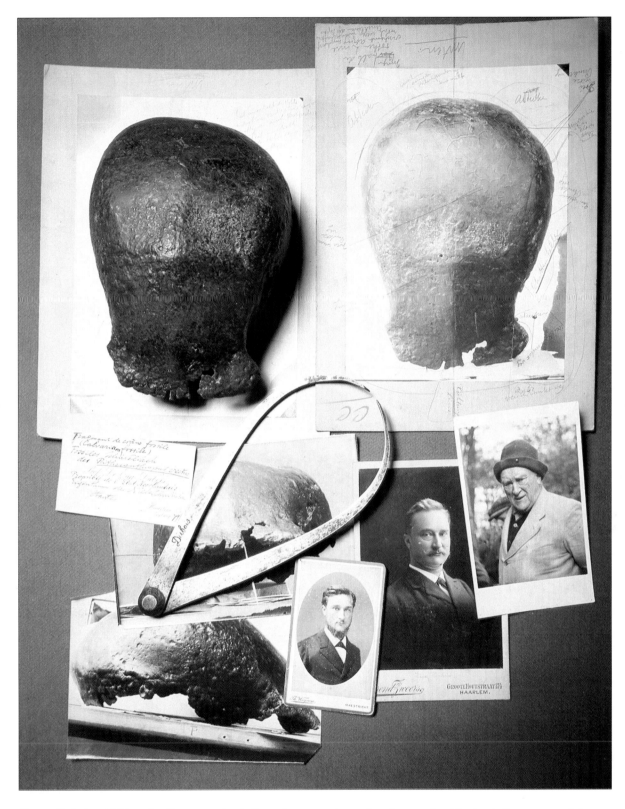

Eugene Dubois, with his major discovery – the skullcap of Java Man. At first this fossil hominid was named Anthropopithecus erectus, *but in the 1950s it was included in the* Homo erectus *group, along with the similar Peking Man. The metal dividers towards the bottom, inscribed with Dubois' name, would be used to measure dimensions and* estimate the volume enclosed by the skullcap, as part of the process of assessing brain volume.

Dubois' first reaction was to regard these finds as being from the same individual – a member of an extinct species of chimp that walked on two legs. He provisionally named it *Anthropopithecus erectus*, "Upright Manlike Ape." Despite further excavations, the team found only one more tooth.

NOT WHAT WAS EXPECTED

By the time Dubois came to publish his descriptions and interpretations of the Trinil finds, in 1894, he had changed his opinion. The erect-walking manlike ape had become *Pithecanthropus erectus*, the "Upright Apelike Man." Dubois had reversed the previous emphasis.

As with the Taung fossil found 30 years later (page 48), Dubois' claims contradicted the climate of opinion. Most authorities believed the big brain, being the prime human feature, would be the first to evolve, atop a still apelike body. *Pithecanthropus erectus*, or "Java Man" as it soon became known, had a small brain but, on the evidence of the femur, a distinctly non-apelike upright stance and gait.

Many experts refused to accept that the fossils came from a human or even a near-human. Some said they were the remains of a giant gibbon or a similar extinct ape. The Upright Ape-Man was ignored or rejected, and the disappointed Dubois finished fossil-hunting in Java in 1895. He moved back to the Netherlands and

MAN-LIKE APE OR APE-LIKE MAN?

Dubois chose the name Pithecanthropus *partly in honor of Ernst Haeckel, who twenty years previously had published a tree of life in* The History of Creation. *In this book Haeckel proposed an as-yet undiscovered Apelike Man,* Pithecanthropi, *as an intermediate evolutionary link between apes and modern humans.*

Haeckel reasoned that speech was such an important feature that it could not have developed as part of the many changes from ape to human. It needed a link of its own. So Pithecanthropus alalus, *"Speechless Apelike Man," would have appeared as the 21st link in the tree. It would have short thin legs, knock knees and "walk but half erect."*

Dubois retained Haeckel's "Apelike Man" Pithecanthropus, *referring to the skullcap that seemed intermediate between apes and humans. Assuming (and a big assumption) that the thigh bone came from the same individual, the creature must have walked upright, hence* erectus.

Right: Dubois" full-sized reconstruction of his "missing link," Pithecanthropus erectus. *It is kept in the Natural History Museum, Leiden, the Netherlands. In his later years, Dubois refused to accept that the fossils being discovered near Peking and in Java again were closely similar to his original finds.*

became Professor of Geology at his old university. He did make a statue-like reconstruction of *Pithecanthropus erectus* based partly on the fossils, with some anatomy borrowed from his own son. But he remained resentful at the reaction of other paleontologists and severely restricted access to his fossils, reportedly even hiding some of them under the floorboards in his dining room.

Dubois continued to hold out against the mainstream of opinion, claiming his fossils represented a true missing link between apes and humans, until his death in 1940. Meanwhile the fossils had been re-examined in the 1920s, and were no longer seen as a brainy ape or a missing ape-human link, but definitely human, although slightly less brainy than modern people. The eminent British anatomist Sir Arthur Keith said of Java Man (as part of a discussion on Piltdown Man): "The thigh bone might easily be that of a modern man, the skullcap that of an ape, but the brain within that cap, as we now know, had passed well beyond ape status." (Recent research indicates that the thigh bone may be relatively young and that the finds are probably not from the same individual.)

FROM PITHECANTHROPUS TO HOMO

Dubois' fossils are now regarded as the first-discovered specimens of *Homo erectus*, an immediate predecessor of *Homo sapiens* that lived in Africa, Asia, and Europe, from 1.6 million to less than 300,000 years ago. The Trinil fossils, along with other Javan specimens and also *Sinanthropus pekinensis* from China (both described below), were renamed as *Homo erectus* in the 1950s, following a systematic "lumping" by the evolutionary biologist Ernst Mayr. Mayr had reviewed the many genera and species that littered the field and cleaned them up into one genus, *Homo*, with only three species. Thus (leaving aside the Neandertals) *Homo erectus* became the first officially named prehistoric species of the human genus *Homo*.

Homo erectus fossils are now known from several sites on Java. Dubois' work was reinstigated in the 1930s by the German palaeontologist Ralph von Koenigswald, who worked mainly at the site known as Sangiran. Dating has shown that the older Dubois fossils are 800,000-500,000 years old, and the rocks and deposits investigated by von Koenigswald at Sangiran were older. In 1938: on the eve of the Second World War his team

recovered a fine skull of *Pithecanthropus* (as it was then still called). The next year von Koenigswald collaborated with Franz Weidenreich, the expert on Peking Man, to show how similar Java Man and Peking Man were.

Indonesian scientists continued the search for fossil hominids after the Second World War. Sites including Ngandong, Modjokerto, Kedungbrubus, Sangiran, and Trinil have been investigated, and the fossils represent numerous individuals of *Homo erectus*. Eleven of the skulls are known as "Solo Man," being younger than those from Trinil and with larger braincases. Overall, Javan *Homo erectus* fossils span several hundred thousand years, and are evidence of how the group changed during this time.

Some fossils from the famous Djetis Beds at Sangiran are less easy to place. They have been variously described as representing an Asian form of *Australopithecus* or perhaps a variant of *Homo habilis*; their age has been claimed to be more than 2 million years. Their standing is controversial. If there were hominids in Asia more than 2 million years ago, did they evolve there and spread to Africa? Or did they originate earlier in Africa and migrate to Asia? Or were these groups living and evolving in their own particular geographical locations?

A street trader (below) peddles illicit herbal and other medicinal wares in Yunnan Province, China. Chinese madicine uses many animal parts and even fossil teeth and bones are sometimes ground up for their supposed medicinal properties. In the 1920s, Western palaeontologists came to suspect that some of these "dragons' remains" were actually of ancient hominids.

DISCOVERIES ON DRAGON BONE HILL

For centuries Chinese folklore has regarded dragons as benevolent creatures. Even their bones, *Lung Ku*, and teeth, *Lung Ya*, are beneficial: they are pulverised and ground up and mixed with a variety of ingredients, to produce potions claimed to have medicinal qualities. Dragon Bone Hill, about 40 miles southwest of Peking (Beijing), was known locally for plentiful teeth and bones - which were in fact the fossils of various, and mostly extinct, large animals. The hill, next to the village of Choukoutien (also written Chou K'ou Tien, Chou-k"ou-tien or Zhoukoudian) was also mined for limestone.

The fossils in the area came to the notice of both the Swedes and the Americans, who were organising expeditions in the 1920s. During these years the Taung find of Raymond Dart in Africa was being ridiculed. Asia was held as the "Birthplace of Mankind", and funds for searches there were in good supply. The rocks around Choukoutien seemed to be of a suitable age for investigation. Through a series of coincidences, and academic and political maneuverings, a Swedish-organised excavation began in the area. The American expedition had to be content with digging in the Mongolian Desert, where the rocks were far too old to hold fossil hominids. (However, they did yield many astounding dinosaur remains.)

Dragon Bone Hill was the site of a huge prehistoric cavern, once lived in by bears. A fossilised human-like tooth was identified by Otto Zdansky, a young Austrian palaeontologist and a member of the Swedish team, in 1921. In 1926, Zdansky described this tooth at a scientific meeting, along with another he had found while sifting through Choukoutien material that had been sent back in crates to Uppsala.

THE CHOUKOUTIEN EXCAVATIONS

In the audience at the meeting was Davidson Black, a Canadian physician and anatomist. In 1918 Black had moved to China and taken the post of Professor of Neurology and Embryology at Peking Union Medical College. He was amazed as he studied the teeth, and arranged with Zdansky to write an article on them, in which he named them *Homo ?sp* (unknown species of the genus *Homo*). Black became involved at Choukoutien, and anthropologists began to watch the search with greater interest.

In late 1927 the team found a third hominid tooth,

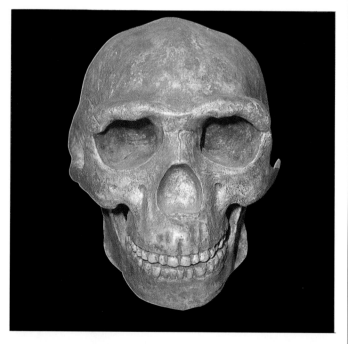

A reconstruction of the skull of Peking Man, the best-known representative of Homo erectus. *Note the protruding bony ridges over the eyes, and the low, sloping forehead. This makes the face look larger in proportion to the whole skull, compared with modern* Homo sapiens.

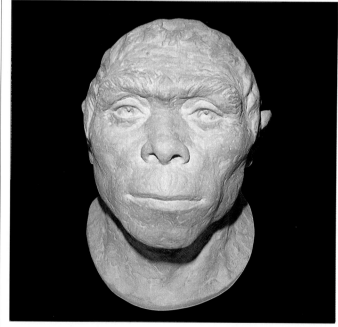

The fleshed-out version of the skull on the left, showing the large, wide face and mouth area compared to the smallish forehead.

Davidson Black led the first teams to investigate the Choukoutien cave system and discovered Peking Man in the late 1920s. His naming of a new genus of hominids, Sinanthropus, on the basis of only one fossil tooth was seen as a bold and inspired move by some experts, and a foolhardy venture doomed to failure by others.

Franz Weidenreich's reconstructions of the fossils of Peking Homo erectus. *The skull at the top displays the characteristic prominent bulges at eyebrow level (facing towards the left), and the slight ridge or keel running from the center of the forehead back over the middle of the cranium.*

which seemed to be from a child and matched Zdansky's second find. Boldly, Black named not only a new species but a new genus from it: *Sinanthropus pekinensis*, "Chinese Man from Peking." The cautious Zdansky was unhappy with this move, but Black saw the very clear similarities between these fossils and those of Dubois from Java. He was supremely confident that the Choukoutien fossils represented an early type of human, and that his proposal would later be substantiated. Eventually it was - but initially many authorities were unimpressed by the rather meagre evidence of a few teeth.

The main excavations at Choukoutien took place in 1927-37. In 1928 half of a lower jaw, with three teeth,

was found. The next year a relatively complete hominid skull was recovered from a part of the cave system by W. C. Pei, a Chinese scientist. This encouraged the palaeontologists and importantly their funders, and work continued in earnest under Black's guidance, until he died in 1934.

In 1935 German scientist-anatomist Franz Weidenreich arrived to supervise the site as Black Successor. By 1937 after years of hard work the Choukoutien team had amassed a remarkable collection of human fossils: 14 skulls, 11 lower jaws, nearly 150 teeth, and about 10 pieces from other parts of the skeleton, chiefly the limbs. Still referred to then as *Sinanthropus pekinensis*, they are now considered fine specimens of *Homo erectus* and dated at about 500,000-250,000 years old - or they would be, if their whereabouts were known today.

THE DAWN OF MAN

THE CASE OF DISAPPEARING FOSSILS

As the Second World War loomed and the Japanese threat increased in China, work halted at Choukoutien in 1937. In 1941, after some persuasion, it was agreed that the fossils would be packed up and shipped to North America for safe keeping, as the Japanese advanced on Peking.

What followed is unclear, but the fossils were never seen again. They may have been lost on the train between Peking and the port of Chinhuangtao (Chinwangtao), or at the port, or even on the steamship *President Harrison*, which was to take them to the United States. Great efforts to trace the remains in the 1970s did not succeed.

Yet Peking Man lives on today, partly through continued excavations after the war by the Chinese, and partly through the work of Franz Weidenreich. He had made a thorough study of Peking Man after Black's death, including many excellent and detailed descriptions, drawings, and plaster casts of the fossils themselves. The only surviving actual fossils from this initial phase of excavation at Choukoutien are the original teeth found by Zdansky, which were taken to Uppsala.

THE HISTORY OF CHOUKOUTIEN CAVE

Since the Chinese resumed work at Choukoutien in 1949, a detailed picture has emerged of the history of the cave and its occupants. The original cavern system was massive, up to140 metres (460 feet) long by 40 metres (130 feet) wide, and 40 metres (130 feet) into the

---

THE EVENING APE

In the late 1920s, as Black announced his find of Sinanthropus pekinensis, *the world of paleoanthropology was especially nervous about extravagant claims based on little evidence.*
In 1922 paleontologist Harold Cook had found a worn tooth in a stream in Nebraska. The director of the American Museum of Natural History, Henry Fairfield Osborn, was involved in defending the right to teach Darwin's theory of evolution in schools, against the views of Biblical fundamentalists. The battle was highlighted by the famous Scopes Trial in Tennessee in 1925. Osborn pronounced that Cook's tooth came from a Pliocene anthropoid, and named it Hesperopithecus – *"Ape of the land where the sun sets," or "Evening Ape" –* haroldcooki. *The popular imagination soon converted this to "Nebraska Man," the earliest American. However, more study and more teeth showed that the fossils were from an extinct species of wild pig. (Pigs have a similar diet, and so similar teeth, to humans.)*

---

highest part of the roof. It seems to have been open to the outside, allowing access by animals and humans for certain periods.

The remains of more than 40 individuals of *Homo erectus* have been recovered from the fossil deposits, which are in places 40 metres (130 feet) deep.

Over 20,000 stone tools have been found, along with thousands of animal bones, many cracked and splintered and some burned. There also seem to be hearth areas where ash and charcoal have accumulated, and plant matter such as large piles of hackberry seeds. (The use of tools and fire is discussed on pages 96 and 98 respectively.)

Choukoutien is the richest *Homo erectus* site in the world. The remains have been awkward to date, but most estimates are in the region of 500,000-300,000 years old. Chinese work suggests the cave shelters were first occupied by *Homo erectus* about 460,000 years ago, and abandoned 230,000 years ago. There are also Chinese claims that the fossils represent people who continued to live and evolve in China, and who were the ancestors of all the Chinese people today - part of the multi-regional hypothesis for the appearance of *Homo sapiens* (Chapter Seven).

CHANGING INTERPRETATIONS

The many remains at Choukoutien have encouraged all manner of interpretation and speculation about the way these humans lived their lives (page 100). The stone tools and the fossils of deer, rhino, and other creatures indicate the inhabitants hunted and butchered large animals, presumably for meat. The thick deposits of ash and the burned, scorched bones indicate a hearth where a fire cooked the meat.

Curiously, many of the *erectus* skulls have their bases missing, around the hole called the foramen magnum, where the brain narrows to the spinal cord and passes down into the neck. Were the skull bases broken deliberately to get at the brain inside, for a tasty meal? Simply smashing open the whole skull would have been less trouble. Perhaps the skulls were de-based as some sort of ritual, or even to make a simple water-carrier! Not only the animal bones have been burned, but some human ones too. Is this further evidence of cannibalism?

Some of this evidence is being reappraised in the light of modern methods and opinions. For example, natural fires and windblown ash can sweep into caves, accumu-

HOMO ERECTUS SITES

Homo erectus *was the first member of our genus* Homo *to spread from Africa. The earliest fossils come from Africa; those from China and South-East Asia are more distinctive, and their skulls would have contained larger brains. Tools of the Acheulean type usually associated with* erectus *have also been found at sites in Africa, Europe and Asia. Some of the younger fossils shown here, such as those from Laetoli, Petralona, Steinheim and Swanscombe, possess a mixture of* erectus *and so-called "archaic sapiens" and even Neandertal features.*

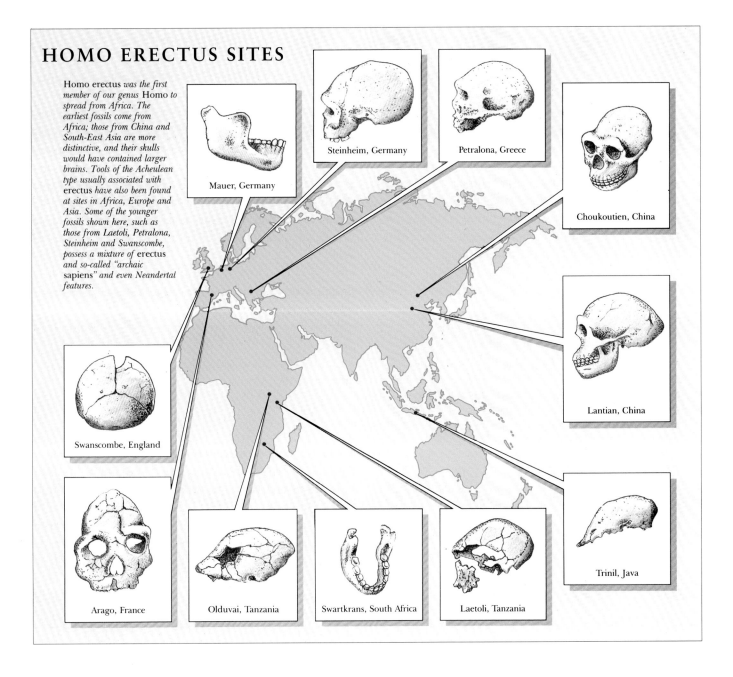

Mauer, Germany

Steinheim, Germany

Petralona, Greece

Choukoutien, China

Lantian, China

Swanscombe, England

Arago, France

Olduvai, Tanzania

Swartkrans, South Africa

Laetoli, Tanzania

Trinil, Java

lations of preserved material such as animal droppings may look similar to ashes and hearths. Bones which appear burned may sometimes be stained by minerals or rotting plants. Carnivores such as hyenas can crack skulls and skeletons, and leave piles of bones in caves. The basal part of the braincase is fairly thin bone compared to the rest of the skull, and could be more easily damaged during preservation.

It has been suggested that at Choukoutien, fire was used only in the latter periods of the cave's occupation. Though the inhabitants hunted for fresh meat, they may have been much less carnivorous than once thought.

Scavenging from carcasses and gathering plant food could have provided the mainstay of their daily diet.

Choukoutien was not completely abandoned by humans around a quarter of a million years ago. In the Upper Cave are remains of *Homo sapiens* some 30,000-15,000 years old.

PEKING ERECTUS PROFILED

A typical member of the Peking *erectus* people would have been nearly 1.5 metres (60 inches) tall, with a well-built physique, and an upright posture and gait like people of today. In fact, apart from the skull, the skeleton was very similar to that of a modern human.

The skull was longer from front to back and lower than the modern human skull. It had pronounced brow ridges, backed by a low, sloping "forehead." The face and lower jaw were less protruding than in australopithecines, but the angular chin so characteristic of today was hardly present. The cranial capacity varied from about 850-1,200 millilitres (30-42 floz) (the modern average is 1,300-1,350 millilitres (45-48 floz).

"Peking Man" is often given the name *Homo erectus pekinensis*, to distinguish these people from other groups of *Homo erectus* such as those from Java and Africa. Compared to the *Homo erectus* finds in Africa, which are 1 million years older (described below), *Peking erectus* had a brain up to one-quarter larger.

EXPANDING HOMINID SKULLS

The general hominid trend through the last 3-4 million years has been towards bigger bodies and proportionally even bigger skulls, which contain relatively larger brains. At the same time, the jaws have shrunk and become less protruding, as shown by these hominid skulls - all from Africa.

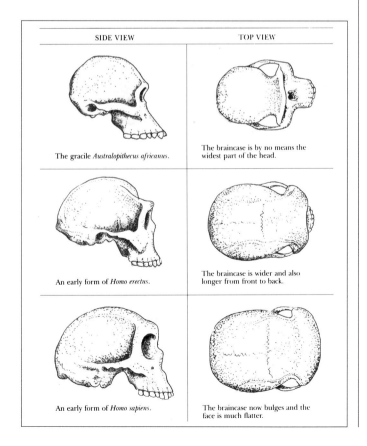

SIDE VIEW	TOP VIEW
The gracile *Australopithecus africanus*.	The braincase is by no means the widest part of the head.
An early form of *Homo erectus*.	The braincase is wider and also longer from front to back.
An early form of *Homo sapiens*.	The braincase now bulges and the face is much flatter.

LANTIAN FINDS

Fossils assigned to *Homo erectus* were found at Lantian (Lan-t'ien) in Shensi Province, China, in 1963-4, by scientists from the Institute of Vertebrate Palaeontology and Palaeoanthropology in Peking. The almost complete lower jaw of a female shows an early example of the absense of wisdom teeth, an evolutionary trait that continues in humans today. It also shows signs of gum disease. There are also parts of a skull and face from a separate location, 15 miles away, but in deposits of the same age, more than 500,000 and possibly 700,000 years old. These fossils may represent an earlier and less evolved type of *erectus* than Peking Man, with an even flatter forehead and bigger brow ridges. Stone tools were discovered nearby.

What may be the most recent remains of *Homo erectus* were located at Dali in China, in 1978. They may be only 200,000 years old. Finds at Hexian in 1980 may date from the same period.

HOMO ERECTUS IN EUROPE

Tools of the type associated with *Homo erectus* in other parts of the world have been found at many locations in Europe. In fact the typical *Homo erectus* tool culture, known as Acheulean, was named after Saint Acheul, a village on the Somme River in France where they were first identified. What are apparently kill sites, with the broken bones of numerous animals as well as Acheulean-type tools, are also known in Europe. These tools and kill sites are described later. However, European fossils of the *Homo erectus* people themselves are less easy to identify.

In 1907 quarry workers in sandpits at the village of Mauer, near Heidelberg in Germany, discovered a fossilised human-like lower jaw or mandible, with teeth (although four teeth went missing). The jaw is big, a match for the largest *erectus* finds from Africa. Remains of animals associated with the jaw indicate that the climate at the time was warm and interglacial (between the ice ages), and other clues point to an age for the jaw of more than 400,000 years.

Opinions vary as to whether the owner of the Mauer mandible, "Heidelberg Man," was a representative of *Homo erectus*. The jaws show some similarities, yet it also has features that can be interpreted as Neandertal. It might indicate that European *Homo erectus* evolved into Neandertal people.

Other fossils of a *Homo erectus-sapiens* nature are from Arago, Bilzingsleben, Vértesszöllös, and Petralona, and are discussed in Chapter Six.

AFRICAN ERECTUS

In the 1950s French palaeontologist Camille Arambourg investigated lakeside deposits of Middle Pleistocene age at Ternifine, on the Agris Plain near Oran, Algeria. In the period 1954–5 three adult lower jaws were discovered, along with primary (deciduous or milk) teeth, and a piece from the side of a skull that may have been of a young child. The lower jaws had the "chinless" configuration similar to the Peking fossils. They are regarded as representing *Homo erectus* and are associated with the typical Acheulean stone-flake and other tools.

In recent years the famed sites of Koobi Fora and the Lake Turkana area have yielded some of the finest, and

The various fossil hominid finds of the past century were generally named by their discoverers according to their view of the find's place in the story of human evolution (and often to immortalise their own names). The fossils were often later reclassified by other experts in the light of new evidence and theories, leading to a confusing multiplication of names. In the 1940s and early 1950s evolutionary biologist Ernst Mayr devised a new system of hominid classification. His inclusion of the various hominids listed here under the label Homo erectus *is now widely accepted.*

oldest, *Homo erectus* fossils. In the 1970s Richard Leakey and colleagues found skulls which bore resemblances to the Peking skulls.

THE WEST TURKANA YOUTH

Then, in 1984, an amazing discovery. On the other side of the lake from Koobi Fora, the fossilised skeleton of a large juvenile hominid was unearthed, almost complete except for the feet, with the bones *in situ*. It was designated WT-15000 and dated at 1.6 million years old, making it one of the earliest confirmed specimens of *Homo erectus*.

Studies on the tooth and bone development of "West Turkana Boy' gave an age of 12 years at death. He was a strapping lad: his height of 1.6 metres (63 inches) would have increased to about 1.8 metres (70 inches) at maturity. The bones indicate a powerful physique.

His skull displayed the distinctive *erectus* brow ridges coupled with a small brain. Compared to *Homo habilis* (Chapter Four) his face, teeth, and jaws were proportionally smaller, his skull longer and lower and less domed, and made of thicker bone. Compared to modern humans, although there are differences in the backbone, hips, and legs, the rest of the skeleton is generally similar.

At Olduvai Gorge, Louis and Mary Leakey found specimens of Homo erectus in the Bed II layers, includ-

HOMO ERECTUS: CLASSIFYING THE FINDS

Year	Popular name(s)	Original scientific name	Current classification	Status
1876	Speechless Ape-Man	*Pithecanthropus alalus*	–	Ernst Haeckel's hypothetical "missing link" in his *The History of Creation*.
1891	Java Man, Trinil Man	At first *Anthropopithecus erectus*, then *Pithecanthropus erectus*	*Homo erectus*	The first fossils of *Homo erectus* to be found, although the contemporaneity of the ancient skullcap and the femur has been questioned.
1912	Piltdown Man, Dawn Man	*Eoanthropus dawsoni*	–	Exposed as a fraud in the 1950s.
1922	Evening Ape, the First American	*Hesperopithecus haroldcooki*	–	Named on the basis of one tooth; further finds by 1928 showed it came from an extinct pig.
1927	Peking Man	*Sinanthropus pekinensis*	*Homo erectus*	Named on the basis of one tooth; discoveries since have confirmed that the Choukoutien cave site is the richest find of *Homo erectus* fossils yet located.
1930s	Sangiran Man	*Pithecanthropus II, III, IV, etc*	*Homo erectus*	Some of the finest and best-preserved skull specimens of *Homo erectus*.
1984	West Turkana Youth	*Homo erectus*	*Homo erectus*	One of the oldest (1.6 million years) and most complete *Homo erectus* skeletons yet excavated.

ing a skull dated at 1 million years old. Associated with these remains are many Acheulean tools, and living floors or areas of occupation – long-buried but, like other parts of the gorge, exposed by an earthquake during the Upper Pleistocene epoch. As *Homo erectus* people strolled along the lakeshores at Turkana and Olduvai, over 1 million years ago, they may have encountered their robust australopithecine cousin, *Paranthropus*. The Swartkrans caves in South Africa, where many australopithecine fossils have been found, also contained *Homo erectus* fossils in the later, upper levels.

THE BABOON AND ELEPHANT KILLS

The presence of *Homo erectus* people has been inferred at several sites, by the discovery of their tools, and the remains of prey presumably killed by them.

About 400,000 years ago there was a lake at Olorgesailie, about 30 miles southwest of Nairobi in Kenya. Field workers have discovered in a small area, about 20 by 12 metres (65 by 39 feet), the fossilised bones of more than 80 baboons, and 10,000 finely made stone handaxes and other tools. They were not today's baboons but an extinct species, big as a female gorilla and with long, fearsome canine teeth.

One interpretation of the evidence is that all the baboons were killed in a relatively short time. This implies co-operation among their hunters. Yet cut marks on the bones suggest the bodies were not butchered in a particularly effective way for meat. And why tackle such large, dangerous opponents in any case? Was there some element of ritual slaughter?

Other kill sites attributed to *Homo erectus* are at Torralba and Ambrona, in central Spain, where the remains are about 300,000 years old. The former con-

Ales Hrdlicka , Czech-born American palaeoanthropologist, criticised the interpretation of Ramapithecus as a human ancestor, and championed the view of Neandertals as a stage or phase in the evolution towards modern humans. In 1923 he examined Eugene Dubois' fossils. He concluded, like many of his colleagues – but not Dubois himself – that the fossils represented an early form of human, and not an ape or an intermediate ape-human "missing link."

tained the fossilised bones of some 50 elephants, and also rhinos, horses, deer, and oxen (although, again, no actual *erectus* fossils). Elephant and horse bones are also present at Ambrona. Yet of all the other elephant remains, there is only one elephant skull, at Ambrona. It seems to be associated with two lines of elephant bones arranged in a T-shape.

How did these sites come about? Possibly the hunters followed or drove wandering herds to a favourite site, where a marsh or similar natural feature acted as a trap.

THE RANGE OF HOMO ERECTUS FOSSILS

The main fossil collections of *Homo erectus* come from Turkana and Olduvai in East Africa, Java, and Choukoutien in China. There are also specimens from Swartkrans in South Africa and Lantian in China. Many *erectus*-like European and Javan fossils are more controversial, as described above. Their ages range from 1.6 million years old in Africa to less than 300,000 years in eastern Asia.

Homo erectus was a considerably bigger creature than *Homo habilis*. In proportion, its brain was slightly larger. The skulls of the early African *erectus* con-

tained brains about 900 millilitres (32 floz) in volume, while later Asian forms reached more than 1,100 milli-liters (39 floz). Other trends are shrinking teeth, especially the rear wisdom teeth.

Cultural evidence for the species, in the form of Acheulean-type tools, spans Africa, Europe, and Asia. It has been proposed that, on existing firm evidence, *Homo erectus* people first appeared in Africa. Possibly they evolved from a population of *Homo habilis*. The species then may have spread from Africa more than 1 million years ago. There seems no need to invoke a rapid large-scale migration, given the long time scale involved. A drift of only a few miles every decade would reach southeastern Asia from Africa in a few tens of thousands of years.

Why are the fossils of *Homo erectus* the first hominid remains to be found outside Africa? A look at the environmental conditions of the time may help to provide an answer – because environment is a vital component in steering evolution.

MORE SPARE TIME?

In this period of changing climate, with its effects on the

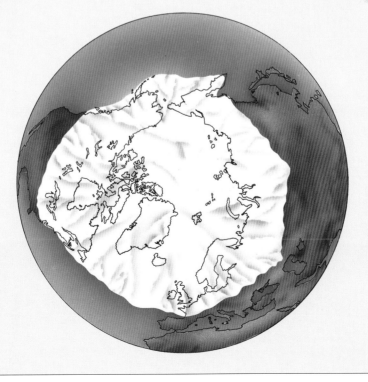

THE WORLD DURING THE PLEISTOCENE EPOCH

The Earth has undergone several major cold periods. The most recent, the Great Ice Ages of the Pleistocene, began about 1.8–1.7 million years ago. Four times, vast sheets of ice spread from the North to cover much of the northern landmasses during the glaciation, then shrank back during the warmer interglacial period.

In Africa and other equatorial regions, the fluctuating climate produced vegetation that varied from warm tropical forests to cooler, drier grasslands. During the cool periods, hardwood forests typical of the mountains there today spread into the lowlands, and the deserts became bigger, at the expense of the lowland jungle.

Farther north, in Europe, central Asia and central North America, average temperatures were at times 7–10°C lower than today. As the ice sheets spread and then shrank, they carried with them on their southern borders the vegetation zones seen as we approach the

Arctic Circle today: temperate forests and grasses, then more cold-resistant coniferous forests, and then treeless tundra.

During the depths of each glaciation, the water locked up as ice meant sea levels fell, at times by more than 100 metres. The world map of sea and land changed and often looked very different from the map of today. There were plenty of extra migration routes between the continents and islands for land animals, including hominids.

The extent of the ice sheet as it spread from the northern polar regions across North America, Europe and Asia.

STAGES IN ACHEULEAN TOOLS

The Acheulean tool tradition includes several variants, or stages. These are sometimes named after the initial identification site. Abbevillian (from the terraces of the Somme River, near Abbeville, France): an early variant characterized by thick, rough-cut hand axes, often with an unfinished butt end which was held in the hand, and only a few flake tools.

Chellean (from the Chelles gravel beds along the Somme River, also discovered in Africa and western Asia): The handaxes had jagged edges and faces with broad flake scars, and there were some crudely knapped flake tools, but the general workmanship was unsophisticated.

Levalloisian (from 19th-century discoveries in the Paris suburb of Le Vallois-Perret): The main flakes were knocked from a core stone which had already been prepared by striking off flakes in a ring around its edge. This formed a circle of 'striking platforms' which the toolmaker could then hit with the hammerstone to remove more, flatter, flakes, and gradually produce a domed shape like a tortoise's shell. Then one well-aimed blow would strike a large flake from the upper part of the dome, leaving the base as a slim, sharp-edged handaxe.

vegetation and the ecology, adaptability would be a key to survival. Tool-making and tool-using, along with the ability to communicate and hunt cooperatively, could have extended the dietary options open to *Homo erectus*. New techniques for obtaining food by scavenging and hunting, might mean less time spent gathering plant food. Analysis of the microwear patterns on *erectus* teeth indicate that meat was becoming a more significant part of the diet, though in what proportions this was hunted fresh or scavenged is not clear.

A shift in diet, with tools speeding up the process of obtaining and processing foods, would mean *Homo erectus* people could spend less time feeding themselves, and more time doing other things. These other activities might include experimenting with tools, developing their social systems, improving their communication skills, and exploring and moving through their surroundings.

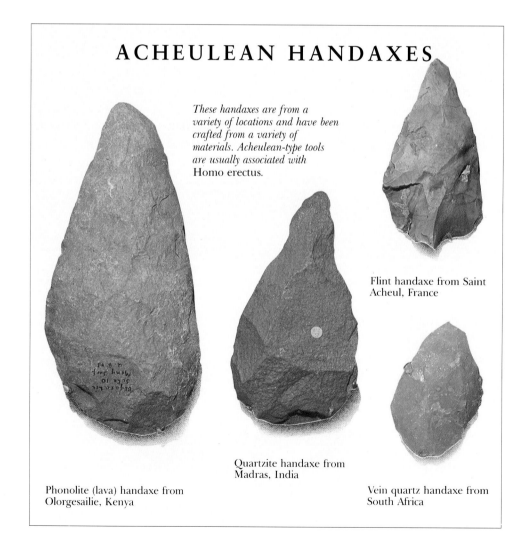

ACHEULEAN HANDAXES

These handaxes are from a variety of locations and have been crafted from a variety of materials. Acheulean-type tools are usually associated with Homo erectus.

Flint handaxe from Saint Acheul, France

Quartzite handaxe from Madras, India

Phonolite (lava) handaxe from Olorgesailie, Kenya

Vein quartz handaxe from South Africa

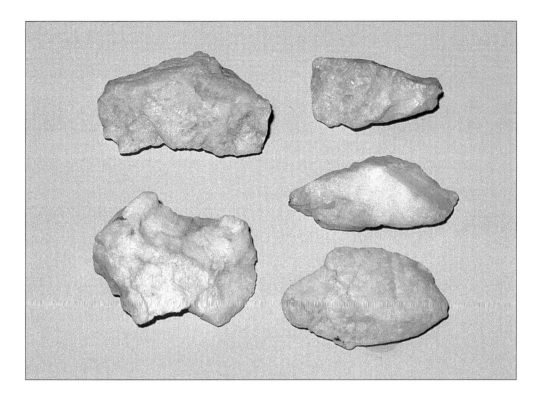

Fragments of quartzite from Choukoutien, shaped by the Peking representatives of Homo erectus. *Thousands of stone tools have been recovered at this productive site.*

As *Homo erectus* colonised cooler regions, another "tool" would become invaluable: fire, for a combination of warmth, cooking, and warding off predators. In the harsh ice-age environment, with food available on a more seasonal basis than in the tropics, improved mental and behavioural abilities would be an important part of the survival kit. The people banded together to gather and scavenge and hunt for food, and for safety in group living, with new forms of food-sharing, communication, co-operation and social organisation in the challenging environment. Evolution may have been affecting "intelligence" as well as physical and biological features, and this was paralleled by an increase in brain size.

TOOLS OF INCREASING SOPHISTICATION

The earliest stone tools may be 2.4 million years old, from Hadar in Ethiopia. Quartz pebbles were deliberately ately shattered and broken to a crude pattern.

Oldowan tools are linked to *Homo habilis* (Chapter Four). Early *Homo erectus* may have used them, too, but the typical tool culture (also called a tool tradition or industry) associated with the *erectus* people is Acheulean. Acheulean tools are a major component of the Paleolithic or Old Stone Age. There are more types, and they are more specialised for certain tasks, and more skilfully fashioned, than the Oldowan versions.

The hallmarks of the culture are no longer cores but flakes. The crudely-edged Oldowan river pebbles were core stones, but many Acheulean implements are based on large flakes up to 20 centimetres (8 inches) long, struck from core boulders using hammerstones or some other hammer. The flakes are the raw pieces for manufacture of "bifacial forms," often called handaxes, picks, or cleavers.

The classic Acheulean tools are handaxes. They may be oval, teardrop or peardrop in shape, or pointed in outline, and they are often flat and broad, with two sharp edges, and shallow scars on the faces where flakes were struck off. The butt end, sometimes smoothly finished, fits into the hand.

The Acheulean toolkit also included the long-edged cleaver, another characteristic implement. In addition there are scrapers, side scrapers, backed knives, small choppers, picks and points and borers.

The earliest known Acheulean tools are about 1.3–1.2 million years old, from Africa. There was a gradual improvement in their design and the quality of their finished workmanship, assuming those that survive were finished. Nevertheless, the basic tools were still broadly the same implements 1 million years after those early examples. In Europe, very similar objects were being crafted only 100,000 years ago.

continued on page 98

HANDS, TOOLS, AND BRAINS

A stone tool, even the most roughly shaped pebble, is the culmination of an intricate network of mental and physical processes. There must be an intelligent brain that can see the need for a tool, and also see the finished tool's shape within the shapeless starting lump of rock. The brain must plan how to fashion the rock, how to hold it, and where to strike it, step by step, to achieve the finished article. Running parallel with this mental ability is so-called motor ability. Motor nerves carry nerve signals from the brain to the various muscles of the body, telling them when to contract or relax. The motor nerve supply to the muscles of the arms and hands needs to be sophisticated enough to tell the dozens of muscles there when to grip lightly or firmly, hold the tool steady, and strike softly or forcefully. And the anatomy of the hand itself must allow a variety of grips, especially the precision grip where the thumb opposes the tip of a finger. In addition, good hand-eye co-ordination is vital since the primary feedback for how the tool is shaping up comes in through the eyes. And from the evolutionary perspective (at least initially), tools must have been useful – if they aided survival in some way, this would encourage their development.

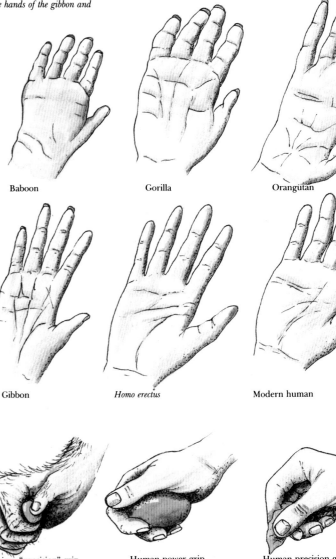

HAND ANATOMY AND GRIP

The human thumb's length and mobility is one key to our manual dexterity. The thumbs of the living apes are relatively short and cannot oppose the fingers so well. The hands of the gibbon and

orang have elongated palms and function chiefly as hooks, for hanging from branches. The chimp has trouble holding an object delicately between its thumb

and its fingertips, in the fine controlled precision grip. It t[...] to clasp the item against the s[...] of its forefinger.

Baboon

Gorilla

Orangutan

Gibbon

Homo erectus

Modern human

Chimp "precision" grip

Human power grip

Human precision grip

TOOL TYPES
Cutting Tools
The thin, sharp edge of a freshly-made stone flake makes an effective cutting tool. It slices with more force if held between the thumb and the flats of the fingers, as shown.

Scraping Tools
The scraper needs a sharp edge, but long and flat, not curved or pointed like the cutter. This early tool may have been used to scrape animal skins for clothing, or to get the last bits of meat from a bone.

Tool-Making Tools
The hammerstone was used to shape another stone, the core, into a tool, or to knock flakes off a core which could then become tools. Another stone, the anvil, may have been used as a base to steady the workpiece and resist blows by the shaping tool.

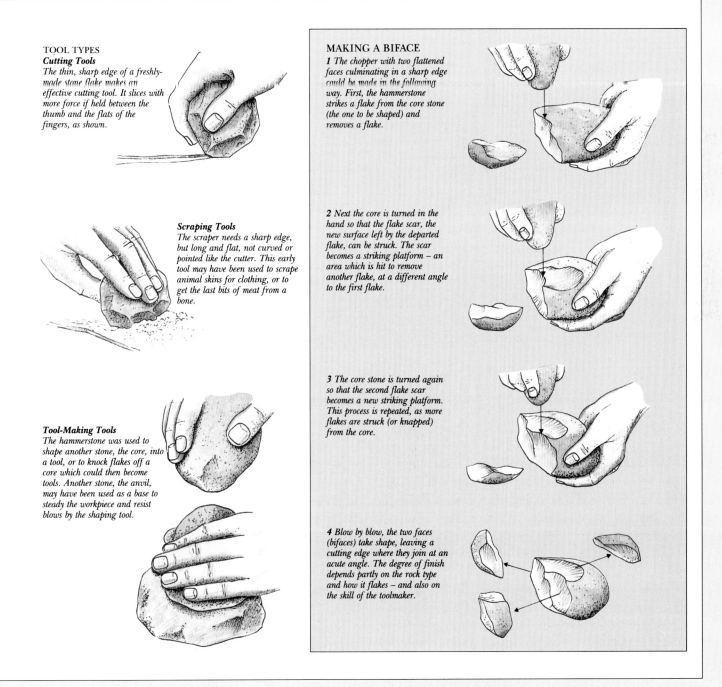

MAKING A BIFACE
1 The chopper with two flattened faces culminating in a sharp edge could be made in the following way. First, the hammerstone strikes a flake from the core stone (the one to be shaped) and removes a flake.

2 Next the core is turned in the hand so that the flake scar, the new surface left by the departed flake, can be struck. The scar becomes a striking platform – an area which is hit to remove another flake, at a different angle to the first flake.

3 The core stone is turned again so that the second flake scar becomes a new striking platform. This process is repeated, as more flakes are struck (or knapped) from the core.

4 Blow by blow, the two faces (bifaces) take shape, leaving a cutting edge where they join at an acute angle. The degree of finish depends partly on the rock type and how it flakes – and also on the skill of the toolmaker.

The obvious use of the tools is for obtaining food, probably scavenged or hunted meat. Cut marks on animal bones from Koobi Fora and Olduvai show that meat-processing may have occurred 1.5 million years ago, presumably using Oldowan tools. Microwear analysis of selected Acheulean tools shows that some may have been employed for animal butchering, some for "woodworking" (perhaps to make wooden tools, shelters, firewood and so on), and some for cutting softer vegetation.

TO BUTCHER AN ELEPHANT

Recent field experiments have shown how the various tools could be used to butcher and process animals as big as elephants. Indeed this practical research indicated that the un-retouched flakes, sharp as when knapped from the core, were very useful: under these circumstances the bifaced core may have been more of an "end product of manufacture" than a vital tool in its own right.

Untouched sharp-edged flakes made excellent knives for preliminary skinning of the tough hide from the carcass. The bifaced handaxe came into its own for cutting through joints, as when slicing through the ligaments and tendons around a shoulder or hip, to remove the limb. Simple pebbles and cobbles sufficed as hammers for cracking bones to get at the marrow in bones or the brain in the skull. Flakes were also well-employed in sharpening wood for digging sticks, pointed spears, or other wooden devices.

The experiments also suggested that although a fresh kill was easier to dismember, the residual flesh left drying and clinging to a carcass, after most scavengers had taken their meals, could be obtained with stone flakes – meat "off the bone." This would be another food resource that was exploitable by hominids with tools, which was unavailable to many other animals. Having hunted or scavenged meat and gathered plant materials, *Homo erectus* may then have cooked them.

FIRE: USE, MAINTENANCE, CREATION

No other animals are as familiar with fire as humans, except perhaps for the family dog. The fossil record is peppered with possible evidence for the use of fire, and this is yet another area of heated debate.

What initial uses could fire have? Warmth, cooking,

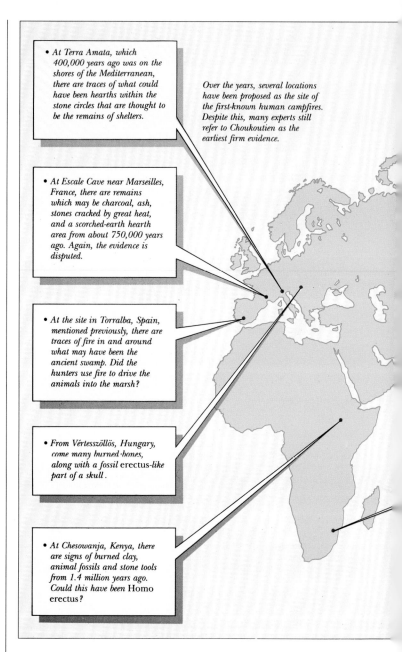

- At Terra Amata, which 400,000 years ago was on the shores of the Mediterranean, there are traces of what could have been hearths within the stone circles that are thought to be the remains of shelters.

Over the years, several locations have been proposed as the site of the first-known human campfires. Despite this, many experts still refer to Choukoutien as the earliest firm evidence.

- At Escale Cave near Marseilles, France, there are remains which may be charcoal, ash, stones cracked by great heat, and a scorched-earth hearth area from about 750,000 years ago. Again, the evidence is disputed.

- At the site in Torralba, Spain, mentioned previously, there are traces of fire in and around what may have been the ancient swamp. Did the hunters use fire to drive the animals into the marsh?

- From Vértesszöllös, Hungary, come many burned bones, along with a fossil erectus-like part of a skull.

- At Chesowanja, Kenya, there are signs of burned clay, animal fossils and stone tools from 1.4 million years ago. Could this have been Homo erectus?

making things, safety from predators, a hunting aid, and an all-round focus to group life have all been suggested. The first widely accepted use of fire is associated with the *Homo erectus* people in Choukoutien cave. But, as so often happens, "use" is loose. Hominid exploitation of fire may have passed through several stages:

being first on the scene after a natural bush fire had roasted and tenderized animal bodies;

deliberately putting carcasses in the way of a spreading natural fire, or putting them onto a confined one;

limiting and feeding a natural fire in some way, as an

CLAIMS FOR FIRE

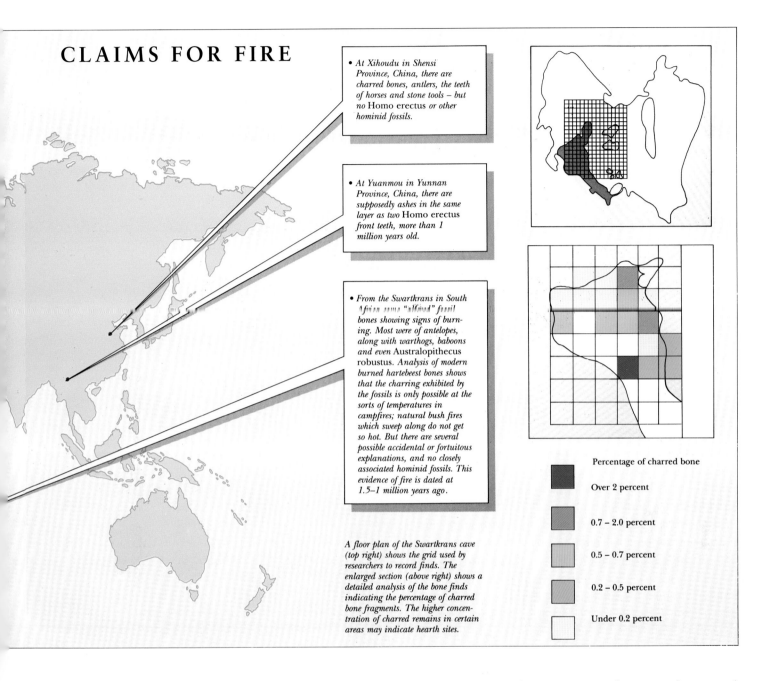

- *At Xihoudu in Shensi Province, China, there are charred bones, antlers, the teeth of horses and stone tools – but no* Homo erectus *or other hominid fossils.*

- *At Yuanmou in Yunnan Province, China, there are supposedly ashes in the same layer as two* Homo erectus *front teeth, more than 1 million years old.*

- *From the Swartkrans in South African cave "altered" fossil bones showing signs of burning. Most were of antelopes, along with warthogs, baboons and even* Australopithecus robustus. *Analysis of modern burned hartebeest bones shows that the charring exhibited by the fossils is only possible at the sorts of temperatures in campfires; natural bush fires which sweep along do not get so hot. But there are several possible accidental or fortuitous explanations, and no closely associated hominid fossils. This evidence of fire is dated at 1.5–1 million years ago.*

A floor plan of the Swartkrans cave (top right) shows the grid used by researchers to record finds. The enlarged section (above right) shows a detailed analysis of the bone finds indicating the percentage of charred bone fragments. The higher concentration of charred remains in certain areas may indicate hearth sites.

Percentage of charred bone

Over 2 percent

0.7 – 2.0 percent

0.5 – 0.7 percent

0.2 – 0.5 percent

Under 0.2 percent

elementary form of maintenance;

transferring a natural fire to a more suitable site such as a cave or cliff overhang, where the rain would not extinguish it, and feeding it to keep it burning;

creating a fire where there was not one before, and fully controlling its size and tailoring its extent for the jobs in hand. The first firm evidence of making fire is only 15,000 years old.

When the Peking *erectus* people lived at Choukoutien, winters were cold and snowy. Fire made it possible to live there. Evidence in the cave includes layers of what appears to be ash from burned-out fires, charcoal pro-

duced from high-temperature burning fires, and scorched stones which may have confined the embers or been put into food or water to heat it up. One layer of ash was 4 metres (13 feet) deep, another 6 metres (19 feet). A concentration of bones and tools around the former layer, along with its quite demarcated limits, may imply that the inhabitants could control and maintain the fire. The simple fact that the fire remained burning in the cave, where it needed managing, points to sophisticated use and signifies intelligent, brains.

continued on page 102

A RIVERSIDE CAMP

Some 400,000 years ago, members of a *Homo erectus* band may have gathered around a fire at Choukoutien cave in present-day China. Some had been scavenging or hunting – animal fossils from the area included cheetahs, hyenas, elephants, horses, sika deer, and woolly rhinos on the plains, and sabre-toothed tigers, leopards, bears, red dogs, wolves, and bison in the wooded areas.

During this time it would have been warm in summer but cold in winter. The cave inhabitants may have draped themselves in animal skins and stayed near the fire for warmth. They may have also used the fire for cooking and to ward off predators. They made a variety of stone tools, and gathered plants such as hackberries for food. They also ate meat, though how much they scavenged and how much was freshly killed is not known. About two-thirds of the animal remains are from deer (whether these were very common, and/or easy to catch and process, and/or especially tasty, is not clear). The large prey animals indicate co-operative hunting and food-sharing – lone hunters would be unlikely to risk tackling a large animal and if they did most of the carcass would have to be left to rot.

At the same time, another band of *Homo erectus* may have been camping by rivers and on beaches at the other end of the Eurasian landmass – at Terra Amata, near present-day Nice, France. The excavations there were led by French archeologist Henry de Lumley, from about 1966. They reveal that rounded huts were built of branches and skins, weighted with beach boulders. There are no fossils of the hominids themselves, but there are numerous Acheulean stone tools characteristic of *Homo erectus* finds elsewhere. Analysis of pollen in coprolites (fossilised feaces) indicated that the site was occupied in spring or early summer. The remains of hearths suggest use of fire, and fossil bones of deer, elephants, and boars are accompanied by shells and fish bones – a prehistoric beach barbecue?

Homo erectus-type hominids survey their temporary riverside camp site by the light of the setting sun. They have constructed a hut resembling the one suggested by evidence from Terra Amata. One group member stands patiently with spear in hand, waiting to impale a fish. Near the hut, a carcass is being butchered, while children play within. The adult on the far right is experimenting with a stone, from which he is striking flakes.

(left) Smoothed Acheulean tools. The split one (top left) shows how one surface is domed, while the other has been flattened. In the absence of the usual measuring scale or geological hammer to give an indication of size, a more modern hand-held tool – a cigarette lighter – suffices in an emergency!

(Right) People in the Sudan build huts from a wooden framework covered with grasses. Such simple methods may have been employed by hominids, such as Homo erectus, at the once-coastal Terra Amata site. There, easily-available stones could have been piled around the base, to strengthen the structure against sea breezes.

AN EARLY SEASIDE CAMP

About 400,000 years ago, while *Homo erectus* people lived at the cave in Choukoutien, another group may have lived in a hut on the shores of the Mediterranean, near Nice.

The sea level of the Mediterranean was 25 metres (82 feet) higher than it is today, and the Terra Amata site is now inland. The climate was also cooler, with firs, pines, and oaks on the lower slopes. On what used to be a pebbly beach are preserved several oval rings of gathered stones, each ring on average 12 by 6 metres (39 by 19 feet), and incorporating holes. The stones may have been the low walls of rudimentary huts. They could act as windbreaks and as stabilisers for the posts and branches stuck into the holes, to form a low conical framework with posts in the centre. The frame would be covered by leafy branches.

There are 11 sets of "foundations" in all. Some encircle signs of what could have been hearths. Associated with them are many Acheulean tools, and the remains of animals such as deer, elephant, rhino, boar, and goat. Some of these fossil bones came from young animals, implying they were hunted rather than scavenged. A

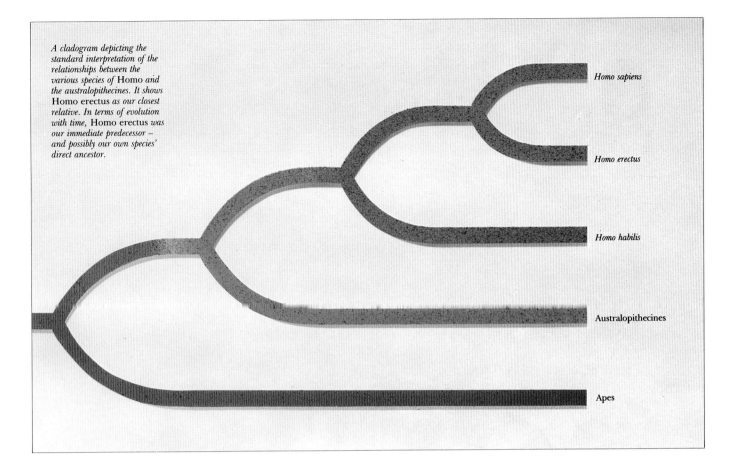

A cladogram depicting the standard interpretation of the relationships between the various species of Homo *and the australopithecines. It shows* Homo erectus *as our closest relative. In terms of evolution with time,* Homo erectus *was our immediate predecessor – and possibly our own species' direct ancestor.*

Homo sapiens

Homo erectus

Homo habilis

Australopithecines

Apes

depression in one hut could have been made by a wooden bowl; there is also yellow-red ocher, a substance commonly used by later people for adornments and paintings of surroundings and bodies.

Much of the Terra Amata evidence is circumstantial. There are no hominid fossils, only one possible footprint, indicating a being 1.5 metres (60 inches) tall. But pollen analysis shows that pollen grains in coprolites (fossilised droppings) came from broom flowers, which flower in spring.

A suggested scenario is that a band of hominids, presumably *Homo erectus*, came to the beach in spring. The size of the huts and the quantities of food remains suggest 20–25 people lived there during each occupation – maybe a hut for each season. As the food ran out or the occupants moved on for some reason, drifting sand and then winter rain covered the derelict hut, packed down and preserved the remains.

THE DEMISE OF HOMO ERECTUS

There are no fossils of *Homo erectus* from less than some 200,000 years ago. What happened to them?

Extrapolating from modern populations of hunter-gatherers, estimates have been made for a world population of *Homo erectus* people of around 1 million. Were they our ancestors? If so, once they had spread across the continents, did the populations in each region evolve into the various *Homo sapiens* groups of today? Or did a select band of *erectus*, perhaps from Africa, become the founding population of *sapiens*, and for the second time was there a continental migration of humans? This is one of the hottest areas of debate in current paleoanthropology.

HUMANS IN
TRANSITION

In 1921, workers at the Broken Hill zinc mine in northern Rhodesia (now Zambia) were digging out a cave. They uncovered what seemed to be parts of a fossilised human skull – although with thicker, heavier facial bones and prominent brow ridges, compared to modern humans. Experts were soon on the scene, and over the following few years, they searched the cave system and the various heaps of spoil and other sites around the mine. They even asked workers to bring in any remains which had been taken home as souvenirs, that could be connected with the find. Sadly, as in similar cases, the nature of the mining and quarrying procedures meant many other fossils had probably been lost or destroyed.

The Broken Hill find turned out to be one of the most complete and best-preserved of ancient human skulls. Along with the "Taung ape-child" (page 50), discovered three years later, it helped to shift the focus of fossil hominids temporarily away from Europe, towards Africa.

In fact the Broken Hill fossils included fragments of bones from at least two skulls, plus two hip bones, and arm and leg bones from possibly three individuals. Studies of "Broken Hill Man" or "Rhodesian Man," as the find was dubbed, indicated the main skull's owner was probably a young man. Its reconstruction gave him a brain size of just less than 1,300 milliletres (45 floz). From the other remains, the length of the tibia (shin bone) put his body height at about 1.7 metres (66 inch-es.)

His teeth were small and badly decayed, which has led to speculation that he ate too much sugary food – possibly honey. And a strange bony nodule on the side of the head could have been caused by a bone tumour, or by infection spreading from the bad teeth. This may have accounted for his death in early adulthood. "Broken Hill Man" could be the first recorded human fatality caused by tooth decay!

TRANSITIONAL FEATURES

The features of the Broken Hill skull seemed to combine those of *Homo erectus*, with its large upper jaw and face, and jutting brows, and our species *Homo sapiens*, with a prominent chin, and a larger brain under a thinner, more domed cranium. A major problem was age: the mixture of rocks and other material in the cave, and the way the fossils had been excavated, permitted only broad dating to somewhere between 300,000 and 100,000 years old. Recent research has narrowed down the date to nearer 150,000-130,000 years before the present.

Since the Broken Hill find, similar fossils with both *erectus* and *sapiens* characteristics have come to light, in Africa, Europe, and Asia. Although they vary in their combinations of features, as a group they are generally regarded as belonging to our own species, *Homo sapiens*. But they are different enough to exclude from our

The Broken Hill skull displays a large facial area relative to the bony case holding the skull, and it lacks the high, domed forehead of a modern human specimen. Also prominent in this exceptionally complete and well-preserved fossil are the heavy, jutting ridges above the eyes. Such features have led some authorities to label it Homo erectus. Others include it in the "archaic Homo sapiens" group, although it may be one of the more archaic of the archaics.

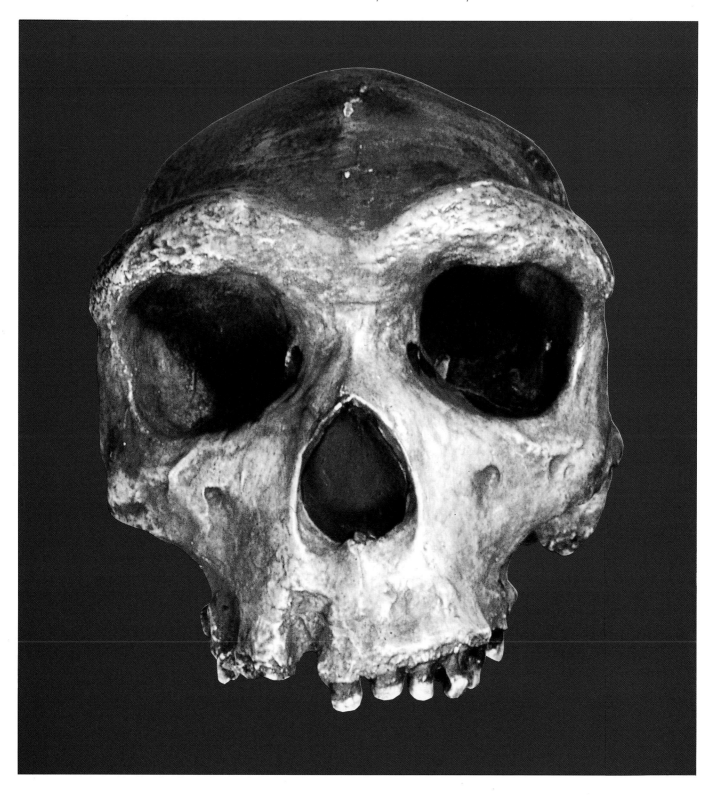

own sub-species, *Homo sapiens sapiens*. They are therefore usually referred to as "archaic" *Homo sapiens*.

ARCHAICS IN AFRICA

At Ndutu in Tanzania, excavators came upon a skull with heavy brow ridges, like the Broken Hill specimen, but possessing a more rounded cranium and signs of a vertical forehead. At Bodo, Ethiopia, another archaic skull came to light, even more heavily built than that from Broken Hill. These two finds are possibly up to 400,000 years old. Another, dated at nearer 350,000 years old, was uncovered in the south of the continent, from Elandsfontein in South Africa. Smaller than the others, and probably from a female, the eyebrow ridges are less marked. Much more recent, and with a domed head showing still other mixed features, is a skull retrieved from the Ngaloba fossil beds of Laetoli. It is estimated to be some 120,000 years old.

Two specimens have also been identified from the productive Omo sites in Ethiopia. "Omo I" has a considerably higher, rounded cranium than other archaic *sapiens* contenders. A piece of the lower jaw shows that its owner had a well-formed chin, another modern attribute. At around 130,000 years old, it is one of the most "modern" archaics yet discovered.

However, from nearby came "Omo II," a specimen with *erectus*-like features. It has a flatter head with a sagittal crest (ridge of bone) running along its centre line, backward from the forehead. These very early members of our own species were seemingly local contemporaries, yet differed considerably in their essential features

ARCHAICS FROM CHINA

During the 1970s, several discoveries were made in China that indicate very early members of *Homo sapiens* lived there at the same time as they inhabited Africa and Europe. "Hsuchiayao Man" is represented by fossils from up to six or seven individuals, first found in 1974. They were excavated from the Hsuchiayao site near Datong, in the mid-Chinese province of Shanxi, not far from Peking (Beijing). Estimated to be 100,000 years old, the fossils are rather fragmentary, but they reveal skulls with rounded backs, a modern and non-*erectus* characteristic.

Another, more complete skull was unearthed at Shaoguan, in the southern province of Guandong, near Guangzhou (Canton). This also had a rounded roof, but with the pronounced brow ridges and thick bone more typical of *erectus*. In 1978 another site in Shanxi, at Dali, yielded a fossil skull with parts of the facial bones intact, and again with a combination of old and new characteristics.

As in Africa, archaic *Homo sapiens* is apparently represented by variants at several places in eastern Asia. This has implications regarding the origins of our own species, and especially of the various modern groups of peoples (Chapter Seven).

ARCHAICS IN EUROPE

In 1960, a fossilised human skull was recovered from a

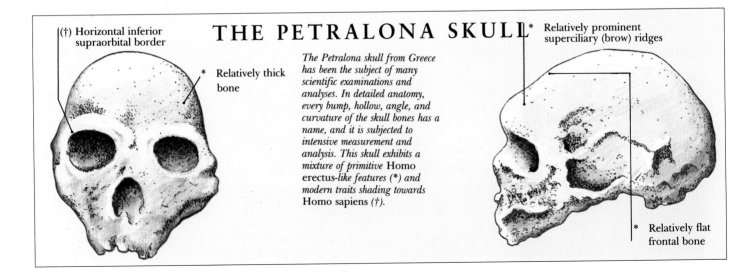

(†) Horizontal inferior supraorbital border

* Relatively thick bone

THE PETRALONA SKULL

* Relatively prominent superciliary (brow) ridges

The Petralona skull from Greece has been the subject of many scientific examinations and analyses. In detailed anatomy, every bump, hollow, angle, and curvature of the skull bones has a name, and it is subjected to intensive measurement and analysis. This skull exhibits a mixture of primitive Homo erectus-*like features (*) and modern traits shading towards* Homo sapiens (†).

* Relatively flat frontal bone

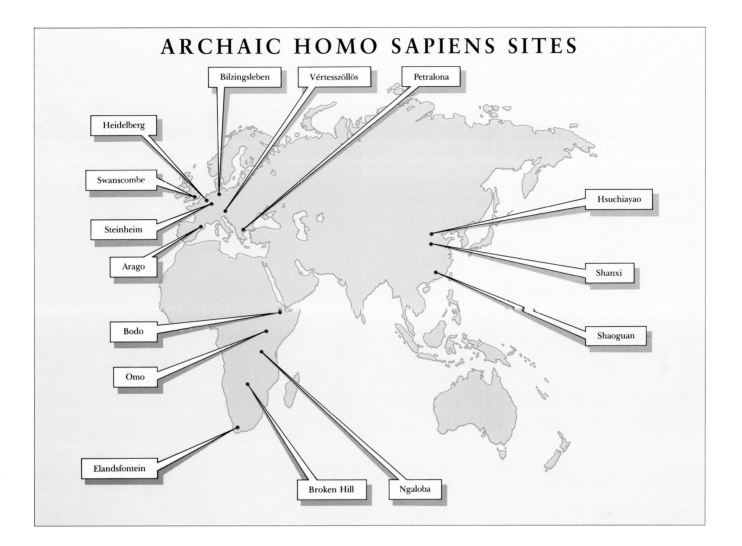

ARCHAIC HOMO SAPIENS SITES

beautiful limestone cave, encrusted with stalactites and stalagmites, in Petralona, Greece. Like the Broken Hill specimen from Africa, it was well preserved and fairly complete, and perhaps as much as 300,000 years old. It, too, showed a mixture of *Homo erectus* and *Homo sapiens* features, and is one of a number of such finds from Europe.

The Petralona skull has a flat, thick, *erectus*-like brain-case, but in other respects it resembles the more modern *sapiens*. In one expert analysis, 21 key physical features were identified on the skull, and fitted into the typical range of such features from either *erectus* or *sapiens*. The score was 6 for *erectus*, 8 for *sapiens*, and 7 indeterminate. On this basis, the owner of the Petralona skull was indeed an intermediate creature. It may have been a very early Neandertal form (page 110).

Further candidates for archaic *sapiens* have been identified in Europe. One is the large Heidelberg jaw.

Another is a set of fragmentary remains, chiefly teeth and part of the occipital bone at the lower back of the skull, from Vértesszöllös, Hungary. French evidence includes the notable Arago finds, consisting of facial bones and bits of skull, jaw, a hip bone, and various teeth, from the south-west of the country. From Germany comes the Bilzingsleben tooth, plus parts of a skull. All of these fossils are extremely difficult to date, but it is likely they are a few hundred thousand years old – roughly equivalent to the African and Asian representatives.

What of the artefacts associated with archaic *Homo sapiens* fossils around the world? Tools include flake cutters, handaxes, worked pieces of bone and wood, and spears. From the general situations of the fossils, we can picture these people as living in caves, or perhaps simply – constructed branch huts.

Where and when did *Homo erectus* finally disappear?

At present, there is insufficient evidence for a clear answer. The overall trend from about 400,000 to 100,000 years ago, is away from the typical *erectus* features towards the archaic *sapiens* types described above.

THE GRAVELS OF STEINHEIM AND SWANSCOMBE

Further archaic-type finds, such as those from Steinheim in western Germany and Swanscombe in southeastern England, pose intriguing questions about another dis-

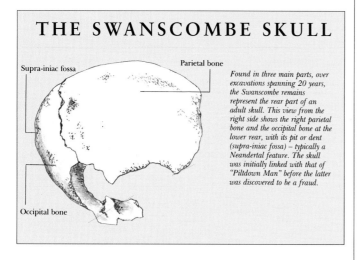

THE SWANSCOMBE SKULL

Supra-iniac fossa

Parietal bone

Occipital bone

Found in three main parts, over excavations spanning 20 years, the Swanscombe remains represent the rear part of an adult skull. This view from the right side shows the right parietal bone and the occipital bone at the lower rear, with its pit or dent (supra-iniac fossa) – typically a Neandertal feature. The skull was initially linked with that of "Piltdown Man" before the latter was discovered to be a fraud.

tinctive group of humans - the Neandertal people. The Steinheim skull came to notice in 1933, and the first Swanscombe remains two years later. They are both probably female and are between 300,000 and 250,000 years old.

The fossilised Steinheim skull was uncovered at gravel pits to the north of Stuttgart. Most of the skull bones are present, but they have been distorted during fossilisation by tremendous pressure from the overlying earth and rock. Studies suggest a rounded dome housing the brain and a flat face (both modern features), but fairly prominent brow ridges.

The Swanscombe skull represents the oldest known Briton. She surfaced from the Barnfield gravel pits around the Kent village of Swanscombe, an area already well-known for Acheulean stone tools. The first clue was part of a fossilised occipital bone from the rear lower portion of the skull, followed the next year by a piece of parietal bone from the left side of the head. Twenty years later, in 1955, further searches recovered a large part of the right parietal bone. Reconstruction of the whole braincase gave a brain volume of 1,325 milli-

The gravels at the Swanscombe site (below). The major find in 1935 was in the beds known as the Middle Gravels. Fossil antlers from an extinct deer are being excavated from the protruding plinth towards the foreground.

liters (46 floz) - approaching modern size. But the front of the skull, including the brow area, face, and chin, were missing.

These remains predated a previous find at Fontéchevade in the Charente region of France, discovered in 1947. Dug from a cave, this consisted of parts of the skulls of two individuals, estimated to be 125,000-80,000 years old, and showing archaic *sapiens* features. Their owners have been variously proposed as forerunners of the Neandertal or Cro-Magnon people described later in this chapter.

The Steinheim and Swanscombe fossils have some hallmarks of archaic *sapiens*. But on further examination, the details of the skull shapes allowed another possibility. In particular the broad, strong occipital bone of the Swanscombe specimen, and its almost bowl-shaped base, with a small dent (the supra-iniac fossa) just above, indicate links with the skulls of Neandertal people. The suggestion is they may represent a "proto-

Stone tools of the Acheulean type found at Swanscombe (above). The area had been famous for many years for the huge numbers of such tools found there, before the skull parts came to light. These are well-shaped handaxes, showing greater sophistication than the less developed Acheulean tools typical of the early Homo erectus *people. The specimen on the right has an untreated, relatively smooth butt end which fits comfortably in the hand.*

Neandertal" phase of human evolution.

The many other finds at Swanscombe include the broken bones of animals, deer antlers, stone tools such as handaxes, and pieces of stone that could be either used tools, broken tools, or tools in the making that had gone wrong. The nature and numbers of these items suggest the following scenario.

One or more groups of Swanscombe people may have camped for some time by the river, accumulating a "garbage dump" of old bones and tools. Their main prey was the now-extinct Clacton fallow deer, which they probably hunted by active pursuit, rather than scavenging. Fragments of rhinoceros and elephant bones could indicate that meat was scavenged from animals which were trapped in the marshes, or killed initially by another predator, or injured by accident. The Swanscombe people would then commandeer the carcasses, dismember them, and transport them back to camp to share.

AN INTERESTING DISCOVERY IN GERMANY

Staying in Europe, the next most recent group of humans is the Neandertalers. The discovery and analysis of their fossils, and the numerous ways they were interpreted over the following years, is a fascinating example of how fashion and reputation, prejudice and personality can affect scientific progress. It is especially illuminating since the early discussions occurred as the theory of evolution proposed by Darwin was being digested by the scientific community.

The Neandertal people were named after the Neander Valley near Düsseldorf, Germany, through which the River Düssel flows (*Neander Thal* is Old German for "Neander Valley"). In 1856 workers were quarrying lime, and they investigated a cave about 20 yards up a cliff-like slope in the narrow, steep valley. Inside, they found a collection of fossil bones in the deep mud of the cave floor. Not recognizing their importance, the quarrymen excavated them but left them jumbled with other debris.

A local teacher became interested in the find and he retrieved part of the top of the skull, along with some of the limb bones. He passed them to the Professor of Anatomy at the University of Bonn, Hermann Schaaffhausen, who concluded that they were probably human and very old. He was particularly struck by the

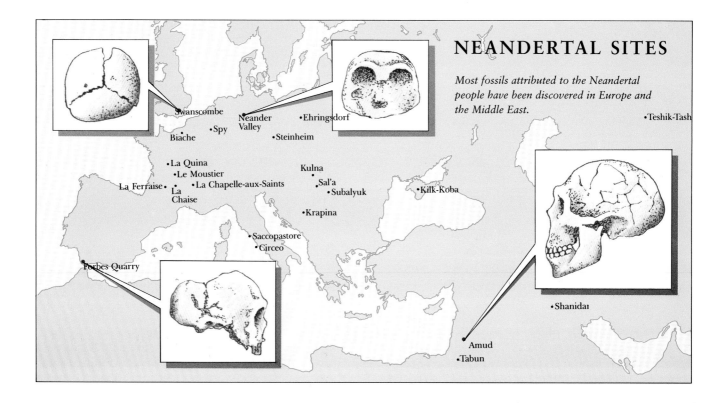

NEANDERTAL SITES

Most fossils attributed to the Neandertal people have been discovered in Europe and the Middle East.

impressive, jutting brow ridges over the eyes, and the thickness and strength of the bowed limb bones, with their large anchorage points for obviously powerful muscles. Schaaffhausen described the find to the Lower Rhine Medical and Natural History Society in Bonn on February 4, 1857. On this day, "Neandertal Man" was born into the scientific community.

THE NEANDERTAL DEBATE

The views then prevailing in the scientific community were not as they are now. It was more than two years before Charles Darwin's *On the Origin of Species* and, by and large, evolution was not on the scientific agenda. Why should people be searching for human ancestors? Another problem was dating: how old were the bones? There were no clues, such as associated animal remains, in the cave, and the various chemical and radiodating techniques we have today were unknown.

The instinctive response of many people was based on the "uncivilised" features of the brow ridges - "characteristic of the facial conformation of the great apes" - the sloping forehead, and apparently stooping posture. Some denied that the remains were human. Others assigned them to some early "wild, brutish, and uncouth" group of subhumans from the far-off past.

Still others held that the bones were very recent, and the bowing of the legs was due to a disease such as rickets.

The German anatomist F. Mayer, Professor at the University of Bonn, declared that the bones were extremely recent. He proposed that they were the remains of a Cossack horseman who had deserted the Russian cavalry as it forced Napoleon across the Rhine in 1814, only some 50 years earlier. General Tchernitcheff's forces had camped in the area during the advance, and the deserter had left his colleagues and hidden in the cave, never to emerge. The bow legs were the result of many hours in the saddle, perhaps compounded by rickets as a child.

Many other experts had their say about the nature of the Neandertal remains. Most emphasised the beetle-brows, the sloped-back forehead and the bow legs: "an individual affected with idiocy and rickets." One French anthropologist held the view that the remains came from "a powerfully organized Celt, somewhat resembling the skull of a modern Irishman with low mental organization." The same physical objects, the fossils themselves, were inspiring all manner of wondrous interpretations.

In 1863, champion evolutionist and "Darwin's bulldog" Thomas Huxley published *Man's Place in Nature*. His analysis of the Neandertal skull was that it was

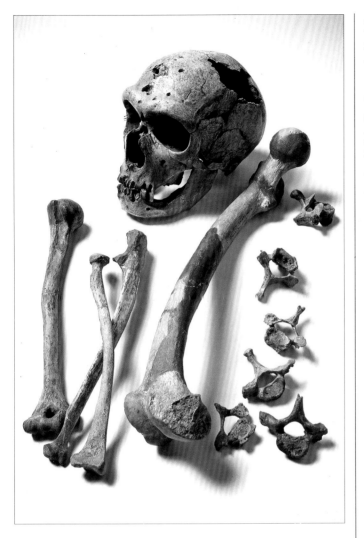

Neandertal fossils found near the village of La Chapelle-aux-Saints in France, in 1908. Compared to a modern human skull, the Neandertal skull has a large face, broad nasal area, and jutting brow ridges. The limb bones such as the humerus (upper arm bone) on the far left were probably deformed in life by a disease such as osteoarthritis. The large central bone is the femur, or thigh bone, with its ball-shaped hip part to the right of the skull. The smaller bones on the lower right are vertebrae (backbones) from the spinal column; they are also misshapen.

human, but seemed to show some retrogressive ape-like characteristics. He emphasised the more primitive features of the fossil, at the expense of the modern characteristics, and wrote: "In no sense can the Neandertal bones be regarded as the remains of a human being intermediate between men and apes." Importantly, Huxley noted that estimates of the Neandertal creature's brain size placed it squarely within the range of sizes for modern humans. If brain size was any indication of intelligence, it was not possible to separate him from us, in this respect. This was one of the first times brain size

had been invoked in the study of relationships between fossil and living humans and apes, and it remains a central characteristic in debates today.

The next year William King, Professor of Geology at Queen's College, Galway, Ireland, proposed an official scientific name for the group to which the Neandertal person had belonged - assuming that the individual was not just an isolated "rickets-deformed pathological idiot." He gave them species status: *Homo neanderthalensis*. In fact King was sceptical of the whole affair, and may have preferred to keep the "cave-man" out of the human genus *Homo* altogether. Giving him separate species status was the next best choice.

Significantly, this was the earliest example of our prehistoric relatives being assigned a formal biological category, with a name to match. It was the start of a profusion of such namings.

NEANDERTAL FROM GIBRALTAR

It soon emerged that the original Neander Valley remains were not an isolated case, or even the first to be discovered. In 1848 a fossil skull from the Forbes Quarry in Gibraltar, found by workers building for the military, had been presented to the Gibraltar Scientific Society. The remains stayed on the Rock, unnoticed in a small run-down museum, until a series of coincidences removed them to the British Association for the Advancement of Science meeting in Bath, England, in 1864. The skull had the prominent brow ridges of the Neander Valley find, but it also showed the facial bones, upper jaw, and teeth. It was officially described by George Busk, Professor of Anatomy at London's Royal College of Surgeons.

In the early 1870s foremost anatomist and Prussian statesman, Rudolph Virchow, added his interpretation of the original Neander fossils. (Virchow studied the cellular progress of disease under the microscope, and is regarded as founding the branch of medicine known as cellular pathology.) Ignoring the Gibraltar specimen, he declared that on "post-mortem" medical evidence, the unfortunate Neander individual had suffered leg-bowing rickets as a child, skull-deforming head injuries in early adulthood, and spine-bending severe arthritis in his later years. Virchow postulated that any ancient, wild, nomadic, hunter-gatherer groups of humans would have been unlikely to look after their old and sick. So this individual must have been a member of a

continued on page 114

THE ENLARGING BRAIN

There has been a basic trend in human evolution towards a big brain. This is not quite so simple as it sounds, because there has also been a trend towards a bigger body. But in general, the brain has grown faster than the body. Both living and fossil apes have a low ratio of brain size to body size (that is, small brain relative to body) - though this ratio is still high among mammals as a group. The relative size of the brain increases among the australopithecines, then through *Homo habilis* and *Homo erectus*, towards the Neandertal people and modern humans.

Not only has the overall size of the brain increased, but the relative sizes of different parts or lobes, in which various functions are concentrated, have also changed. For example, in the living great apes the occipital lobe at the rear of the brain, involved in vision, is quite large. In living humans it is relatively small. The reverse applies to the parietal lobe - dealing with body awareness, including touch and other skin senses - and the temporal lobe, which is important in memory and "higher" mental functions.

Evidence from fossil skulls and cranial endocasts (page 49) indicates that the earliest hominids, the australopithecines, showed a more human-like than ape-like brain organisation. The major innovation which they possessed over apes was bipedality - walking on two legs. It is possible that a relatively enlarged parietal lobe was coupled with the more sophisticated muscular co-ordination, balance and mental concentration required by this mode of movement. Once the brain had become so modified, the way was open for acquisition of other feats relying on mental/physical coordination, such as using and making tools, and various forms of vocal communication.

BRAIN AND SPEECH

Could early hominids talk? Fossil evidence can give a few pointers. For example, a fossilized Neandertal hyoid bone (part of the voicebox apparatus) shows no significant differences from our own. A reconstructed head and neck of Homo erectus *(above right) is sufficiently like that of a modern human (below right) to indicate that vocal sounds similar to our own may have been possible, though perhaps in a slower and less finely tuned fashion. Fossil hominids also possessed a distinct part of the brain, Broca's area, which is a type of "speech centre" and which is absent in apes (shown in the modern human brain, below). However, speech and language are so much a part of culture, and heavily involved with other mental faculties, that no firm conclusions can be drawn.*

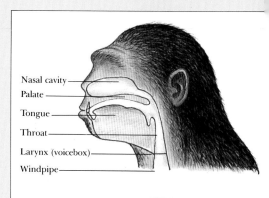

Nasal cavity
Palate
Tongue
Throat
Larynx (voicebox)
Windpipe

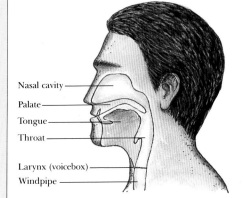

Nasal cavity
Palate
Tongue
Throat
Larynx (voicebox)
Windpipe

Modern human brain

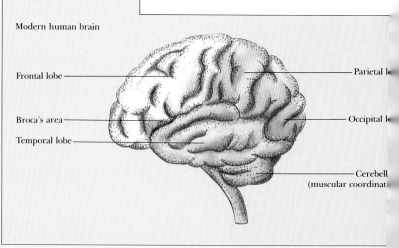

Frontal lobe
Broca's area
Temporal lobe
Parietal l
Occipital l
Cerebell
(muscular coordinat

BRAIN SIZE AND SHAPE

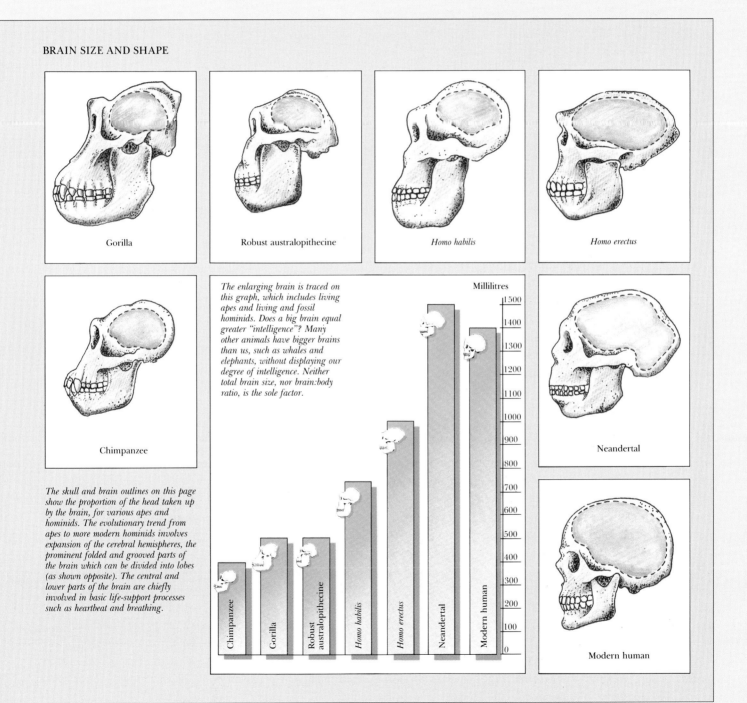

Gorilla

Robust australopithecine

Homo habilis

Homo erectus

Chimpanzee

The enlarging brain is traced on this graph, which includes living apes and living and fossil hominids. Does a big brain equal greater "intelligence"? Many other animals have bigger brains than us, such as whales and elephants, without displaying our degree of intelligence. Neither total brain size, nor brain:body ratio, is the sole factor.

Millilitres

1500
1400
1300
1200
1100
1000
900
800
700
600
500
400
300
200
100
0

Chimpanzee

Gorilla

Robust australopithecine

Homo habilis

Homo erectus

Neandertal

Modern human

Neandertal

Modern human

The skull and brain outlines on this page show the proportion of the head taken up by the brain, for various apes and hominids. The evolutionary trend from apes to more modern hominids involves expansion of the cerebral hemispheres, the prominent folded and grooved parts of the brain which can be divided into lobes (as shown opposite). The central and lower parts of the brain are chiefly involved in basic life-support processes such as heartbeat and breathing.

more settled and civilised agricultural-type society – and thus the remains must be relatively recent. Virchow opposed the theory of evolution, which was gradually gaining ground in mainstream science, and he was one of the last authorities from the Darwinian era to express such views forcefully.

THE CARICATURE CAVEMAN

In 1887, two fairly complete Neandertal-type skeletons turned up near Spy, Belgium. In 1908 a spectacularly complete skeleton was excavated from near La Chapelle-aux-Saints, France. Reconstructions of its owner were made by Marcellin Boule at the Museum of Natural History in Paris, around 1908-12. These reinforced the impressions given by Huxley, and a popular image emerged of the archetypal "caveman" shuffling along with splayed toes, bent knees, stooping back, and slouching shoulders, from which the head protruded forwards in an uncouth manner. Boule maintained that although the skull housed a brain perhaps as big as a modern person's, the parts of the brain involved in intelligence and intellect were not well developed.

Sure enough, in life, the La Chapelle individual would probably have walked with a pronounced stoop, because he was an aged individual with severe arthritis, particularly in the spine. Strangely, several of Boule's interpretations were not consistent with the actual fossils. In the 1960s, further study and reinterpretation of the evidence and the La Ferraise remains overturned many of his conclusions, to give the modern view of the Neandertal people as described here.

Yet, at the time, the picture of a dim-witted, shuffling caveman was readily accepted by many fellow scientists. Professor of Anatomy at the University of London, Grafton Elliot Smith, wrote of Boule's "clear-cut picture of the uncouth and repellent Neandertal Man...The heavy overhanging eyebrow-ridges and retreating forehead, the great coarse face with its large eye-sockets, broad nose, and receding chin, combined to complete the picture of unattractiveness, which it is more probable than not was still further emphasised by a shaggy covering of hair over most of the body." (Of course, the fossils bore no evidence of hair or other body covering.)

The reasons why these conclusions gained so much favour are complex. They involved rivalry between different groups of researchers, each espousing its version of human evolution, some within the clerical tradition

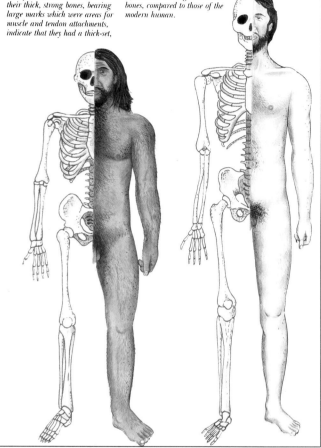

NEANDERTAL AND MODERN HUMANS

Most Neandertal people were not as tall as modern people of European descent. However, their thick, strong bones, bearing large marks which were areas for muscle and tendon attachments, indicate that they had a thick-set, *stocky and powerful physique. Note the heavy construction of the Neandertal thigh and shin bones, compared to those of the modern human.*

(such as Boule) who may have wished to preserve the creationist view of modern humans, and some without. There was an undertow of opinion that the primitive, ape-like "Neandertal Man" could not possibly be a suitable ancestor to modern, civilised humans, as some evolutionists were suggesting at the time. Therefore, emphasising his brutish qualities and belittling his resemblance to modern humans would serve to put the Neandertal on a sideline of human evolution, which led it to "deserved extinction."

Since these controversial beginnings, fossils and other evidence of Neandertal people have been found at dozens of sites in Europe. Gradually more discoveries were made and the Neandertalers extended their range eastwards, as far as Teshik-Tash in Uzbekistan, and south to what are now Israel and Iraq in the Middle East, and North Africa.

NEANDERTAL SKULL

Compare the profile of this representative Neandertal skull, from about 60,000 years ago, with the Cro-Magnon skull on page 123. The facial bones and the mandible (lower jaw) are relatively large. Despite the low forehead, the brain space inside some Neandertal crania was as big, or bigger, than that inside many modern crania. This is partly due to its long front-back measurement.

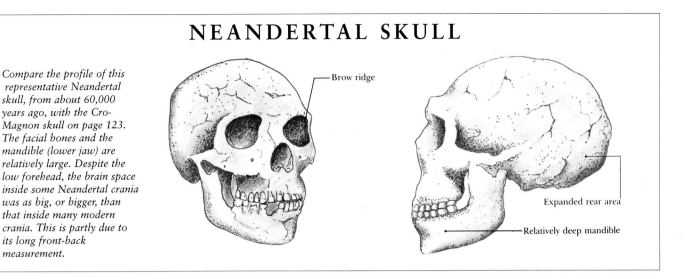

Brow ridge

Expanded rear area

Relatively deep mandible

THE NEANDERTAL AGE

When did the Neandertal people live? Fossils of the "typical" representatives are dated from 70,000 to 35,000 years ago. This was the time when ice advanced from the north, down across much of Europe, during the penultimate great Ice Age. One of the latest Neandertal specimens from Saint Cezaire, France, could be as little as 31,000 years old. Several features of the Neandertal skeleton indicate a body adapted to cold-climate survival (see below).

Discoveries pertinent to their distant past have been made in France and Wales. In 1976, parts of a skull and jaw were recovered from a site at Biache, and estimated to be more than 100,000 years old. The lower rear of the skull has the projecting Neandertal-type shape. (This may be connected with anchorage of the neck muscles.) Other French finds at La Chaise and Lazaret support this evidence, and suggest that Neandertal people were living in Europe more than 130,000 years ago, another time of ice and cold.

From 1978, bits of teeth and jaws were found at Pontnewydd, a Welsh site of roughly the same age as Swanscombe. The teeth show similarities with those of typical Neandertalers. Taken with the Swanscombe and Steinheim evidence, they could indicate people with Neandertal features living in Europe more than 200,000 years ago.

A NEANDERTALER DESCRIBED

Reconstructions from the various fossilised bones and teeth of Neandertal people give a good idea of their size and build. A typical adult was about 1.6 metres (64 inches) tall and weighed 70 kilos (155 pounds) - short-

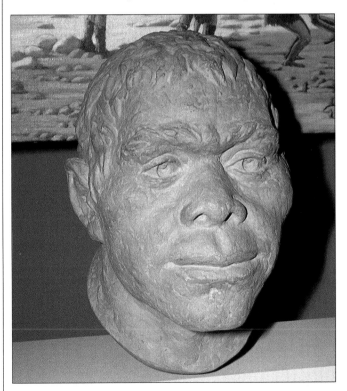

In this reconstruction of a Neandertal person as he may have looked in life, the nose is squat and broad, the cheeks and mouth area relatively large, and the eyes seem deep-set beneath prominent brow ridges. The forehead is low and sloped back, so that the top part of the skull looks less domed than that of a modern human.

The mountains of central and southern Europe, such as the Stubai Alps in Austria, have long, cold, snowy winters with a brief summer thaw. During the Ice Ages of the past million years, lower overall temperatures would have meant this type of climate occurred at much lower altitudes. For thousands of years, permanent ice sheets covered much of northern Europe.

er than today's Europeans, but stockily built. He or she had strong, thickset bones, large and firm joints, powerful muscles, a long trunk, and relatively short legs, especially in the calves. The posture was upright, as in ourselves, and not stooped and shuffling as in the earlier reconstructions.

Estimates of brain size for the Neandertal people are mostly above 1,300 millilitres (46 floz), and up to 1,700 millilitres (60 floz) in some large males. This is in the same broad range as for humans of today, and up to 10 percent bigger when taking into account the ratio of size of brain to body.

In the head region the forehead receded, the promi-

nent superciliary brow ridges arched over the eyes, and the face jutted forwards. The overall shape of the skull was low and long from front to back, with a bulge already mentioned, the "occipital bun," at the lower rear of the skull, above the neck. In the facial area, the size of the nasal aperture and cavity indicate a large, protuberant nose, while grooves in the bone for blood vessels suggest that the face received a good supply of blood. There was a mid-facial prominence and lack of a chin.

These characteristics are consistent with adaptation to a cold climate. The thickset body with small but powerful limbs would have a lower surface-to-volume ratio than a tall, thin, long-limbed design. This could help to conserve heat. (Similar features exist in some groups of people today, such as the Inuit of the far north.) A large nose and nasal cavity would have warmed the icy air before it reached the lungs, while the rich blood supply to the face helped to prevent frostbite when this area was exposed.

TOOLS, CLOTHES, AND OTHER ARTEFACTS

The tools associated with typical Neandertal fossils are of a type known as Mousterian, named after the Le Moustier cave in the Dordogne region of France, where they were first recognised and described. They include knives, spear-heads, cleavers, chisels, borers, and scrapers, mostly made from flakes chipped off a large "core stone." The core was selected for its hardness and splitting qualities, and the flakes struck from it were then finely chipped ("knapped") to the final cutting edge. Such workmanship indicates a high degree of intelligence and manual dexterity.

A general picture emerges of Neandertal people living in small groups, hunting for meat and also gathering food plants. Evidence of fire, in the form of charred bones and hearth remains, occurs at many sites. In the bleak tundra of ice-age Europe, especially during the intense cold period of 60,000-40,000 years ago, fire would have helped survival by keeping low temperatures and marauding predators at bay, as well as being useful for thawing food and cooking. The Neandertal people were probably able to hunt and roast large animals such as deer, wild ox, cave bears, mammoths, and woolly rhinoceros. They may have used animal skins in a rough-and-ready way for clothing, and possibly to make tent-like shelters. And they seemed to have cared

(Above) A reconstructed skull of a Neandertal person, housed in the Rijksmuseum in The Netherlands. It is based on the famous fossil specimens from La Chapelle-aux-Saints (page 111).

for their old and sick. Some fossils are remains of individuals who were so diseased or aged that they would have been unable to fend for themselves.

Caves figure largely as sites of Neandertal fossils. This may be partly because the Neandertalers lived in them, sheltering from the bitter cold, ice, and thick snow. It is also because, as the evidence suggests, they buried their dead there. And this seems to have been carried out with some form of ceremony or ritual. This is the first known evidence of humans indulging in ceremony.

NEANDERTAL FUNERALS

Possible burial sites occur across the Neandertal range, from La Ferraise, Le Moustier, and La Chapelle-aux-Saints in France, to Kiik-Koba near the Black Sea, south

continued on page 120

THE FLOWER FUNERAL

The earliest palaeontological and archeological evidence for ritualistic and ceremonial behaviour is associated with Neandertal people. It concerns human burials. Across their range, remains of Neandertalers young and old have been found carefully arranged in grave sites, often with associated items such as stones, bones, and horns placed in specific positions.

At La Ferraise rock shelter in the Dordogne area of France, the headless remains of a child were discovered in what would have been a narrow shallow pit. The body was in a flexed posture. Nearby is another child's skull, but it has no jaw. The bones of a Neandertal child at the Teshik-Tash site seem to have marks on them which could have been made by stone tools. Were these juveniles mutilated as part of some ceremony concerning the fate of their soul, and their journey into a life after death?

Some of the most exhaustive excavations have been carried out at the Shanidar cave in the Zagros Mountains of present-day Iraq, where a fascinating selection of Neandertal fossils has been uncovered. Some of the individuals were injured or diseased during life, and they would only have survived with care from others. Microanalysis on the soils in the cave reveal pollen grains from grasses, trees, and wild flowers, which presumably drifted into the cave, or were brought in by animals or the Neandertalers themselves. Strangely, the analysis pinpointed concentrated clusters of pollen grains which seemed to be positioned around one of the skeletons, Shanidar IV. These fossils are dated at some 60,000 years old. The grains came from cornflowers, yarrows, ragworts, thistles, grape hyacinths, and other colorful flowers, and there is also evidence of woody horsetail. One interpretation is that the Neandertal was laid to rest among the flowers, perhaps on a "bed" of green woody horsetail, or the flowers were scattered on his body. Ceremonies of this type take place daily in our modern world.

A Neandertal family holds a ceremonial burial for one of their elders. They have prepared a shallow pit in the shelter of a cave mouth, and laid the body to rest within. Draped in animal skins to keep out the intense cold, they place bones and scatter petals in the grave. Such burial rituals could indicate concern for the departed person's soul and a possible belief in an afterlife.

*A preserved baby mammoth is unearthed in the Susuman
district near Magadan, eastern Russia. The Neandertal and Cro-Magnon
people would have encountered these huge relatives of elephants on
many a hunt, and they may have cooked mammoth steaks around the
camp fire. This particular baby died about 10,000 years ago.*

to Tabun and Amud in Israel and Shanidar in present-day Iraq, and east to Teshik-Tash near Tashkent.

At this last site, a shallow pit had been dug for the purpose. Ibex horns seem to have been arranged around the head of the dead person, who was probably a boy, and there is a charred area which could have been a graveside fire. At Le Moustier, the arrangement of fossil bones and artefacts indicates that an adolescent boy had been carefully placed on his side. His head rested on a "pillow" of flints, and a stone axe and charred bones were adjacent. This burial dates from about 50,000 years ago.

At Shanidar, pollen analysis suggests that flowers or other plants were placed over the body, as "grave gifts," 60,000 years ago. Skilled analysis of one of the skeletons shows that the owner was probably blind in one eye, and had a malformed arm. In an Italian find, a cir-cle of stones surrounds the fossil skull, suggesting a ritual.

These various decorations and gifts, along with traces of what may have been food, could mean that the Neandertal people held some type of superstitious or religious beliefs, and even the concept of an afterlife.

WHAT HAPPENED TO THE NEANDERTALERS?

After about 30,000 years ago, Neandertal remains are conspicuously absent. Presumably these people died out. Why? In Europe, their disappearance occurred soon after a new type of human appeared. These were the Cro-Magnon people, known from their fossils to be anatomically fully modern *Homo sapiens sapiens*, and physically almost indistinguishable from people of today.

There are various proposals concerning the disappearance of the Neandertal people. One is that they did not in fact die out - they evolved with great rapidity into the Cro-Magnons. This proposal has come in and out of favour over the years. It is supported by some

Searching for Neandertal fossils in the caves of Palestine in the 1930s. As first it was thought that the Neandertalers lived only in Europe. Subsequent discoveries of their fossils, some with mixed Neandertal-modern features, pushed their range southeast to Israel and east into the Russia.

Neandertal fossils that supposedly show modern features, and a few Cro-Magnon-type remains that display certain Neandertal characteristics. But the picture is not so simple. In the locality of Saint Cezaire, the later Neandertal inhabitants were contemporaries of the earlier Cro-Magnons. This overlap means the later Neandertal people, at least, could not be ancestral to the early Cro-Magnons.

Recent research from Israel adds more data for consideration. Fossils of modern humans from Jebel Qafzeh, near Nazareth, have been studied since 1935. They are admittedly somewhat "primitive," with slight brow ridges and other features. They have been dated by new advanced techniques, such as electron spin resonance (ESR) and thermoluminescence (page 20), at 100,000 years old. Neandertal remains from the Kebara cave, on Mount Carmel, are much younger - about

60,000 years of age.

There are two other well-known cave sites on Mount Carmel. At Tabun, Neandertal-type fossils were previously believed to be 45,000 years old. Animal teeth from the same level of excavation have also been dated recently, by ESR, to 120,000 years old. A few hundred yards away is the cave of Skhul, with modern-type fossil humans formerly estimated at 40,000 years of age. The new dating techniques on associated teeth give an age of around 100,000 years. So Neandertal and modern people lived in the same area at almost the same period, with little sign of one evolving into the other, or with enough time for it to happen. Nevertheless, future discoveries and technical advances could radically alter the picture, once again.

Evidence from tools is also inconclusive. The typical Neandertal tool culture is Mousterian, while the main culture of the early Cro-Magnons in Europe is the considerably more sophisticated Aurignacian. However, at Saint Cezaire, some of the tools associated with fossil Neandertalers seem to combine Mousterian and more advanced features. Conversely, at Jebel Qafzeh and

Skhul, the fossilised human skulls of the modern type are associated with basically Mousterian tools.

EXTINCTION BY EPIDEMIC

Another proposal centres on extinction from disease. Assuming the Cro-Magnon people came to Europe from elsewhere, they may have brought with them diseases to which the Neandertalers had no resistance. Similar events have occurred during recorded history. When Europeans travelled to the Americas in the 16th century, they introduced diseases such as smallpox, measles, diphtheria, influenza, and whooping cough to the largely non-resistant inhabitants. Historians estimate that tens of millions of native American peoples died as a result.

A further possibility is that the Neandertal people may have suffered "passive displacement" by the more highly-organized and better-equipped Cro-Magnons. The newcomers were superior at hunting, gathering, finding shelter, and generally surviving. They out-competed the Neandertal people, who succumbed through lack of food and shelter.

Yet another version is that the displacement was not passive but active. The Cro-Magnons killed off the Neandertal people. It is fascinating to speculate, but firm evidence for one or more of these proposals is still awaited.

SUB-SPECIES OR SPECIES?

What of the Neandertal people's status and position on the "tree of human evolution"? For some decades, many authorities have regarded them as a distinct subspecies, *Homo sapiens neanderthalensis*, of our own species. More recently, some experts have argued that they are sufficiently different not only from modern humans *(Homo sapiens sapiens)*, but also from our overall species *Homo sapiens*, and that they deserve their own species status: *Homo neanderthalensis*.

For example, at the Israeli sites mentioned above, Neandertal and modern people lived in the same localities, around 100,000 years ago. Yet the fossils from nearby Kebara, 40,000 years later, show no sign of combined or merged characteristics - they still retain their distinctive Neandertal features. And modern human fossils from the same area, 30,000 years old, show no Neandertal influence. If the two groups could not

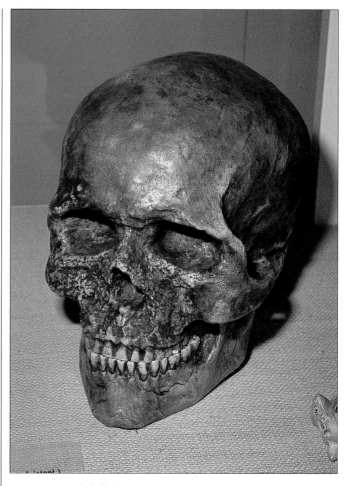

A reconstructed skull of a Cro-Magnon person, housed in the Rijksmuseum at Leiden in The Netherlands. It is based on the original specimens from the Cro-Magnon rock shelter in the Dordogne, France. Compared with the Neandertal reconstruction shown on page 117, it has a smaller facial and nasal area, and a higher domed forehead.

(rather than would not) interbreed, this could fulfil one of the criteria for calling them separate species. It would also mean that the Neandertal people were not subsumed by breeding into larger groups of modern humans.

As to their position, it seems likely that Neandertal people were not on the main evolutionary line to fully modern humans. Both these groups may have developed from a common ancestor, more than 200,000 years ago. A cold-adapted people, the Neandertalers evolved further in ice-age Europe, surviving successfully until their relatively sudden end, without large-scale merger into *Homo sapiens sapiens*.

THE CAVE IN THE DORDOGNE

The 1860s were an exciting decade. In 1868, as the world debated Darwin's *On the Origin of Species* and the nature of the Neandertal fossils, French workers were building a road near the village of Les Eyzies, in the Dordogne region. They chanced upon a cave-like rock shelter containing bones virtually identical to those of people today, yet dating from 30,000 years ago. Along with the bones and teeth were finely-worked stone tools and other objects, and signs of campfires. The name of the site was Cro-Magnon, and the discovery opened another chapter of human evolution.

Subsequent finds of similar bones, teeth, and artefacts have been made at many sites, right across Europe, particularly at Chancelade and Le Solutre, also in France; Grimaldi in Italy; Predmost and Dolni Vestonice in Czechoslovakia; and in the Middle East and North Africa. The name Cro-Magnon is now usually applied to all such peoples, who appeared fairly rapidly in the region about 40,000-30,000 years ago. They are includ-

A selection of flint spearheads from Paleolithic -Old Stone Age times. Their sites and tool types are Moravia (Solutrean), Kent's Cavern (Solutrean), Gower Peninsula, Wales (Aurignacian), and Dordogne (Solutrean). The Solutrean industries date from about 20,000-15,000 years ago.

ed within our own modern sub-species, *Homo sapiens sapiens*. They continued to thrive through the last great Ice Age to the end of the Pleistocene epoch, 10,000 years ago, when the climate warmed. The many discoveries have given us extensive knowledge of what the Cro-Magnon people looked like, a good idea of how they lived, and how they differed from the Neandertal people before them.

A typical Cro-Magnon male was more than 1.8 metres (70 inches) tall, a woman more than 1.65 metres (65 inches). They stood erect, with straight limbs. Muscle anchorage sites and other features of the bones show that they had a powerful physique. Their skulls lack brow ridges but have a chin, a flat face (though slightly broad by today's standards), a vertical forehead and a domed braincase. To paraphrase an anthropological saying: given a good wash, modern clothes, and modern behaviour, "Cro-Magnon Man" would pass unnoticed on any city street.

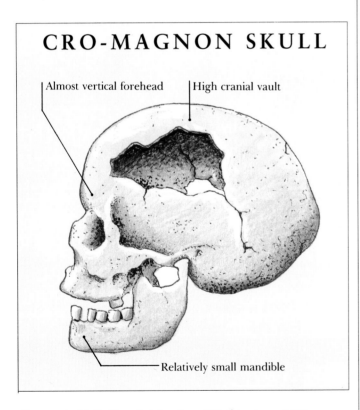

CRO-MAGNON SKULL

Almost vertical forehead

High cranial vault

Relatively small mandible

Compared with the Neandertal on page 115, this representative Cro-Magnon skull from the period 30,000-20,000 years ago has a more vertical forehead and a higher, rounded "vault" to the main braincase. It lacks the prominent eyebrow ridges which would have given a Nenadertal face its "beetle-browed" appearance.

TOOLS OF INCREASING VARIETY

The tools of the Cro-Magnons showed great advances over those of Neandertal people. They were beautifully made in stone, bone, and wood. Many of the stone implements were based on long, narrow pieces called blades, struck from a larger prepared "nucleus." These

continued on page 126

A STAY AT THE SEASIDE

During Cro-Magnon times in Europe, the climate was still cold, and tundra or steppe vegetation covered much of the land. Yet the people adapted well to these harsh conditions. Indirect evidence from their sculptures and paintings shows that they wore cloaks and clothes of animal hides sewn together, and sometimes decorated with beads. They sheltered in caves or built tents from branches, leaves, and animal skins. They were chiefly nomadic, hunting meat and gathering plants while based at a site with a nearby water supply, and moving on as necessary.

One of the richest Cro-Magnon sites is in Dolni Vestonice near Brno, Czechoslovakia, which has been investigated since 1923. Remains of fires and hearths have been carbon-dated to about 25,000 years old. Among many tools and worked objects are a small female statue (possibly a fertility symbol), and pieces of clay, ivory, bone, shell, and teeth fashioned into pendants, beads, and a model of a human head. The tents or huts at Dolni Vestonice probably had an inner conical framework of branches, a covering of skins, and rows of upright bones and tusks reinforcing the lower edges, to keep out the cold and wind. Near the huts was a domed hearth with many hundreds of clay lumps, apparently in the process of being moulded into animal shapes and fired. It could be a prehistoric sculptor's workshop.

The Cro-Magnons hold a position of prominence in our general perception of human prehistory. This is partly because they were one of the first people whose fossils and artefacts were thoroughly investigated in a scientific fashion. Also, much of the work was carried out by Europeans, and from a relatively Eurocentric viewpoint of the world. It has become clear that, as the Cro-Magnons lived in Europe, many other groups of modern humans were evolving sophisticated cultures around the world. It will be some time before a global picture emerges of this phase of prehistory.

Cro-Magnon hunters return to their beach camp somewhere in Europe, on a morning more than 20,000 years ago. Pieces of fish and deer meat are cooked over the fire and shared with the children. Some group members are planning to spend the day foraging for food along the shore, while others intend to work on new stone tools.

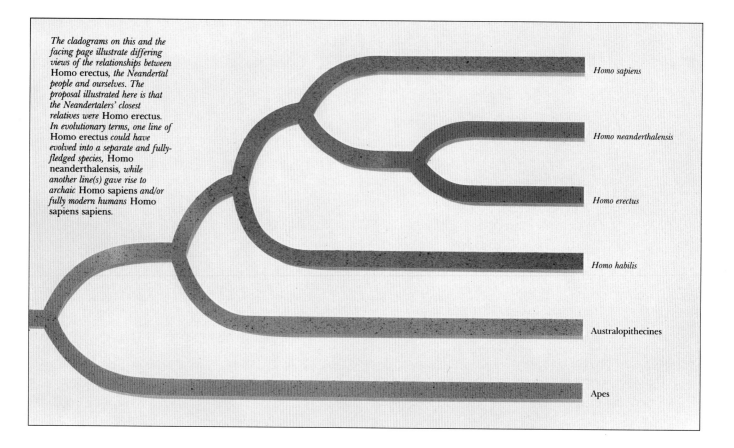

The cladograms on this and the facing page illustrate differing views of the relationships between Homo erectus, the Neandertal people and ourselves. The proposal illustrated here is that the Neandertalers' closest relatives were Homo erectus. In evolutionary terms, one line of Homo erectus could have evolved into a separate and fully-fledged species, Homo neanderthalensis, while another line(s) gave rise to archaic Homo sapiens and/or fully modern humans Homo sapiens sapiens.

Homo sapiens

Homo neanderthalensis

Homo erectus

Homo habilis

Australopithecines

Apes

were shaped and sharpened either by direct striking with a hammer of stone, bone, or antler, or by indirect percussion, using the hammer to hit an intermediate "punch" of antler or bone, which was applied to the workpiece. Cro-Magnon tools included spears, leaf-shaped spearheads, and spear-throwers; points with double barbs; double-edged knives, "backed knives" with one blunt edge for gripping; borers and scrapers, and fishing hooks and barbed harpoons.

One important type of tool was the chisel-like burin. This came in various designs and was used to shape bones, antlers, ivory, and wood - not only to make other tools, but also for carved and sculpted objects of art. The earliest evidence of prehistoric art dates from Cro-Magnon times. The carvings, engravings, moulded clays, sculptures, and paintings were remarkable new cultural developments marking a giant leap forward (described in the next chapter).

The earlier types of Cro-Magnon tools, common around 30,000 years ago, are termed Aurignacian. Their later tool "industries" include the Solutrean, from around 20,000-17,000 years ago, and the Magdelenian, at about 15,000 years old. These various industries belong to the Upper Paleolithic phase, or Upper Old

Stone Age. (The Mousterian tools of the Neandertal people are from the Middle Paleolithic stage.)

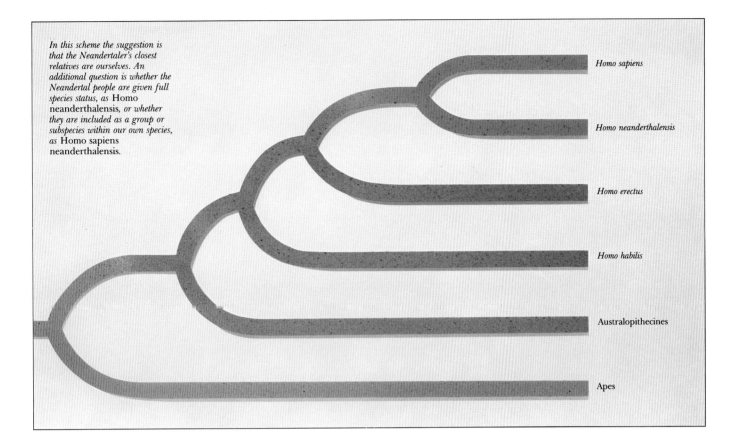

In this scheme the suggestion is that the Neandertaler's closest relatives are ourselves. An additional question is whether the Neandertal people are given full species status, as Homo neanderthalensis, or whether they are included as a group or subspecies within our own species, as Homo sapiens neanderthalensis.

Homo sapiens

Homo neanderthalensis

Homo erectus

Homo habilis

Australopithecines

Apes

HUNTING TECHNIQUES

Cro-Magnon people were proficient hunters. Around the Dolni Vestonice camp are deep piles of old animal bones, mostly mammoths. More mammoth remains, representing perhaps 600 of these extinct elephant relatives, occur at Predmost, along with the remnants of tents. The remains of some 10,000 horses were uncovered at Le Solutre, in France. Other prey were reindeer and woolly rhinoceros. The great numbers of prey animals could indicate that each Cro-Magnon group had many mouths to feed. Perhaps more likely, the hunters trapped large herds of prey in ravines or made them stampede over cliffs. Then they cut up the meat, skins, and bones at their leisure.

The picture of Cro-Magnon life is well-established. These people are prominent in our history because they were the first of their kind to be scientifically discovered and investigated. Yet evidence of modern humans from similar times, from 50,000 years ago, has now been unearthed in many parts of the world. Where did these people come from?

CHAPTER

THE
EMERGENCE OF
MODERN MAN

When the Cro-Magnon people entered Europe, more than 30,000 years ago, they had already evolved into anatomically modern humans. Physically, they would have been indistinguishable from Europeans of today. Where and when had the change occurred, from whoever were their predecessors, into the fully modern *Homo sapiens sapiens* they represented? This was the final stage in our physical evolution. During the 1980s, evidence from palaeontology, anthropology, genetics, and linguistics has once again swung the focus of attention toward Africa.

Some of the most eyebrow-raising studies involve mitochondria, minute sausage-shaped structures inside many kinds of living cell. Mitochondria are energy-converters, changing basic energy-containing substances into chemicals which the cell can use more easily. They are important in human evolution because they contain one form of deoxyribonucleic acid or DNA.

DNA makes up the genes which are inherited by offspring from their parents. The main genes are the nucleus or "control centre" of the cell and are made of nuclear or nDNA. During reproduction, nDNA from mother and father comes together, and is mixed and shuffled to give a unique gene combination for each offspring. Sometimes the DNA changes, or mutates, and new genes appear.

Mitochondrial DNA – mtDNA or mDNA – is not inherited from both parents, but only from the mother. The much smaller amounts of mtDNA compared to nDNA, and its simpler mode of inheritance, make it a useful substance for genetic study.

THE MTDNA CLOCK

In the 1980s Allan Wilson, Mark Stoneking, and Rebecca Cann, from the University of California at Berkeley, compared samples of mtDNA from people around the world, who were representative of various regional or racial groups. The aim was to find out by how much mtDNA differed among the groups. This could give some idea of the closeness of the relationships of these groups of people alive today. The more similar their mtDNA, the more closely related they are. The idea of a "molecular clock" assumes that mutations in mtDNA crop up at a known and regular rate. If this is true, it should be possible to work back and estimate how long it was since two samples of mtDNA diverged from the common ancestor. The mtDNA of humans as a group has also been compared with our closest relatives, the chimps. It is assumed that humans and chimps last shared a common ancestor 5 million or more years ago. The amount of mtDNA divergence which has occurred since helps to "set" the molecular clock.

MITOCHONDRIAL EVE

The mitochondrial DNA studies have thrown up some remarkable conclusions. Computer-constructed relatedness trees show the least number of mtDNA mutations required to bring about the observed diversity. The fewer mutations, the closer the relationship. A greater "genetic distance" indicates a common ancestor further back in time. The results showed that people from different parts of Africa have most diversity in their mtDNA. This suggests that modern humans have been living there the longest, giving enough time for these DNA changes to occur.

Further calculations came to the startling conclusion that all modern people have the same origin – a relatively small population of humans who lived in Africa perhaps 200,000–150,000 years ago. This notion is sometimes referred to as the "African Eve" or "Mitochondrial Eve" hypothesis. All anatomically modern people, *Homo sapiens sapiens*, including ourselves and groups like the Cro-Magnons, can trace their history back to this time. *Homo sapiens sapiens* spread from this small and discrete origin to take over the world. This proposal has become known as the "Out of Africa" model of modern human origins.

The analysis of the mtDNA information makes certain assumptions, and both these and the conclusions have provoked enormous debate. For example, the degree of similarity between two samples of mtDNA genes can only indicate relatedness if the shared genes came from the same ancestor, rather than appearing by chance. And populations of people who become separate, undergo mtDNA changes, then mix and interbreed again, can alter the results. The arguments are technical, and opinions have evolved since the original scientific publications on mtDNA and "Eve" in 1987. Since then, the same type of analysis on nuclear DNA, and on the biochemicals it codes for in the body, have seemed to support the Out of Africa scenario. But there are also other alternatives.

EVOLUTION IN SITU

The multi-regional model proposes that modern humans evolved gradually from ancient humans in many parts of the world. The ancient humans may have

Camels cross the parched desert sands of the Middle East. In the past these hoofed mammals were employed for milk, wool, skins, and meat, as well as being beasts of burden; today they are as likely to be involved in racing. In the distant past, it is possible that the first anatomically modern humans spread through the Middle East towards Europe and Asia, more than 100,000 years ago. The fluctuating climate of the Ice Ages meant that the Middle East area was not always so arid as it is today.

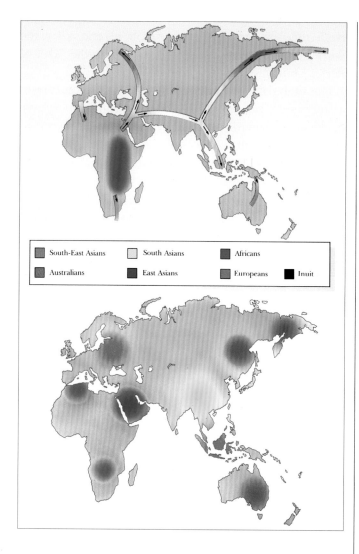

South-East Asians   South Asians   Africans

Australians   East Asians   Europeans   Inuit

suggestion, a small modern human population appeared in one place and then spread, and the differences would then appear as the various modern groups settled in new regions, presumably within the last 100,000 years or less.

The debate continues, partly because the fossil evidence can be interpreted to support both proposals.

FOSSILS OF THE PAST 150,000 YEARS

Some of the fossil evidence for the recent phases of human anatomical evolution is described in the previous chapter. Significant fossils include remains from Omo, and Klasies River and Border Cave in South Africa.

The Omo and Border Cave fossils are difficult to date because of the circumstances in which they were found. The Klasies River remains, pieces of skull, jaw, and limbs, are more firmly dated at 100,000–80,000 years old. But they are fragmentary. Some experts say they are of modern humans, and that there is increasing evidence for fossils of anatomically modern humans 100,000–70,000 years ago in southern and eastern Africa. Combined with fossils from the Israeli caves (page 121), they indicate that anatomically modern *Homo sapiens sapiens* lived in South Africa and the Near East 100,000 years ago. Perhaps the "ancestral Eve population" came from between these two regions, in East Africa.

Other experts dispute the interpretations of the fossils and the conclusions. Meanwhile, the most recent specimens are still being dated and debated.

ANCIENT TO MODERN

In the Out of Africa scenario, presumably the spreading modern humans would take their physical characteristics with them. Yet supporters of the multi-regional proposal point to fossil evidence from many regions, notably Asia, which shows gradual change from very ancient to fully modern, with no outsider features intruding. For example, in Indonesia, the original Java Man of Dubois (Chapter Five) could be seen to grade into the remains found at Ngandong in Java, which show bigger brains but a similar mixture of features to Java Man. The line can then be traced to the earliest human fossils from Australia, again showing a similar combination of features, at less than 50,000 years old.

been *Homo erectus*, or archaic *Homo sapiens,* or other groups.

This proposal suggests that in each region, people gradually evolved from ancient to modern. For example, today"s inhabitants of southeastern Asia may have evolved from Java Man, and present-day people in the north-eastern Asian region from Peking Man. Modern Europeans could be derived from an intermingling of Neandertal people, and others who migrated to Europe from elsewhere – possibly the Near East. One exception may be North and South America, where already-modern people arrived within the last 50,000 years (see page 132).

The multiregional model has many important implications. It would mean the differences observed today in native groups of peoples, in physique and hair type and skin colour, have a much longer evolutionary history – perhaps 1 million years or more. In the Out of Africa

If the Eve scenario did occur, yet the available fossils

(Opposite) In the "Out of Africa" proposal (top) the first anatomically modern people evolved in sub-Saharan Africa, 150,000–200,000 years ago. In the multi-regional proposal (bottom), groups of ancient humans independently evolved roughly in parallel (below).

Did ancient ancestors of the Australian Aboriginals (below) evolve for hundreds of thousands of years almost in situ, or did they spread from Africa into the area within the past 100,000 years?

from outside Africa do not show any typical African anatomical features, this could mean the Out-of-Africa people did not intermingle and interbreed with the local inhabitants as they spread. Does this mean that they, and so us, are a different species from archaic *Homo sapiens*?

A tree of relatedness for various human biochemicals, coded for by the DNA in the cell nucleus. The African groups are more closely related to each other, and like-wise groups from other regions. This implies support for the Out of Africa "Rapid Replacement" scenario (see page 132). A new population appeared in one area (Africa) and then spread, replacing any other human groups on the way.

POPULATING THE WORLD

Two of the world"s major land masses (apart from frozen Antarctica) seem to have acquired their anatom-ically modern human inhabitants last. These are Australia and the Americas.

The first people may have reached Australia as long as 50,000 years ago, on rafts from southeastern Asia. Puzzlingly, skulls 25,000 years old of early Australians exhibit much variation; some are thin-boned and light-ly-built, others are sturdy and robust. Do these differ-

ences indicate different origins, distinct geographical groups, or males and females of the same species?

THE FIRST AMERICANS

Archeological evidence once showed that there were no good signs of human occupation in the Americas before about 12,000–11,000 years ago. This is the "Clovis Barrier", named after stone tools found near Clovis, New Mexico. These tools have a characteristic fluted structure, the spearpoints and arrowheads being grooved to fit into a notched wooden shaft. The last glaciers were retreating from north-central North America at the time of the Clovis people, and the stone tools have been found associated with the bones of great ice age mammals that roamed the area.

Recent studies question the Clovis Barrier. Some are archeological, and controversial. The Meadowcroft rock shelter near Pittsburgh may have been occupied 14,500 years ago. Remains of cremated humans and animals from a cave at Monte Verde, in southern central Chile, have been dated at 12,000 years old. Charred wood and what might be flake and core stone tools have been assessed at more than 30,000 years old. Cave art from the Piauí region of Brazil may be 30,000 or more years old. If people lived in South America then, they must have been in North America much earlier.

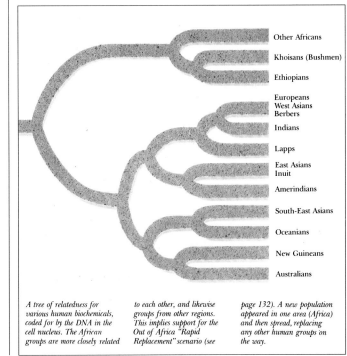

Other Africans

Khoisans (Bushmen)

Ethiopians

Europeans
West Asians
Berbers

Indians

Lapps

East Asians
Inuit

Amerindians

South-East Asians

Oceanians

New Guineans

Australians

A tree of relatedness for various human biochemicals, coded for by the DNA in the cell nucleus. The African groups are more closely related *to each other, and likewise groups from other regions. This implies support for the Out of Africa "Rapid Replacement" scenario (see* *page 132). A new population appeared in one area (Africa) and then spread, replacing any other human groups on the way.*

TEETH AND MIGRATIONS

We do not all have teeth of the same shape. In the field of dental anthropology, the teeth of living people and fossil teeth are studied and compared. Patterns of tooth anatomy emerge. These are largely inherited and remain stable for long periods, because teeth do not vary so widely or evolve as rapidly as certain other body features that are subjected to natural selection.

Two overall tooth patterns have been identified in indigenous Asians and native Americans. The sundadonts are from southeastern Asia, Indonesia and Polynesia. The sinodonts come from east and northeastern Asia, and North and South America. There is a characteristic combination of features defining each group. Sinodonts tend to have an extra root (making three in total) on the first lower molar tooth, and extra ridges on the inner surface of the upper incisor, which give it a "shovel" appearance.

This dental anatomy is another line of evidence that all native American peoples came from northeastern Asia. Teeth from human remains show that the sinodont pattern evolved in northeastern Asia perhaps 20,000 years ago, or even before, in present-day China and Mongolia. (This pattern is present in the Upper Cave humans from Choukoutien, Chapter Five.) Dental anthropology is also being used to study the migrations of people from south-eastern Asia through Indonesia and to the Pacific islands.

HISTORICAL LINGUISTICS

Linguistics is the scientific study of language. There have always been elements of looking into the past, not only at the earliest written records, but also at how the different languages spoken today have arisen. Languages, like living things, have evolved (though much faster), with ancient tongues splitting and dividing into newer versions. Like animals and plants, languages can be classified and organised into related groups, and their origins traced on an evolutionary tree.

There are about 5,000–6,000 distinct languages around the world today. These can be grouped into more than 200 families. One of the best-studied language families is Indo-European, which embraces extant groups like Armenian, Albanian, Celtic, Italic, Germanic (which encompasses English and German), Baltic, Slavic, Iranian, Indic, and Greek – plus extinct languages such as Anatolian and Tocharian.

Linguists analyse spoken languages and propose reconstructions of the "protolanguage" from which they evolved. The words of protolanguages can reveal much about the people who spoke them, and their societies, and the objects and concepts significant in their lives.

Similarities and differences among the languages of the Indo-European family point to a protolanguage last uttered by people some 7,000–6,000 years ago. Its geographical origin has been variously identified as Europe or the Russian steppeland. Recent research suggests it may have been an area between the Caucasus Mountains and ancient Mesopotamia. By the "Dawn of History" some 4,000 years ago, this protolanguage had fragmented into a dozen or more branches, and so on, to the present day.

THE MOTHER TONGUE

In the past few decades, some linguists have been pushing back the time boundaries. Traditional techniques compare two or a few languages, check that their similarities are truly due to a shared common ancestor, and

Making poison for arrow tips in the Ituri forest region of Zaire, West Africa (below). The Out of Africa proposal implies that the earliest groups of modern Homo sapiens sapiens could have been established in Africa by 100,000 years ago. The differences observed today, between various geographical groups of modern humans around the world, would have arisen after this time. The multi-regional or "Regional Continuity" proposal (as opposed to Rapid Replacement) implies that such differences have a much longer history – perhaps a million years or more.

work back to reconstruct root words and syntax (these methods are akin to cladistic analysis in biology). One of the new techniques is multilateral comparison, which compares many languages at once. It has been criticised as being insensitive to chance similarities, but it has thrown up many new ideas.

One novel notion, a great talking point among linguists in the 1980s, is that the existing language families can be grouped into seven and ten superfamilies. The Nostratic super-family (meaning "our language"), for instance, would include Korean, Altaic, Indo-European, Kartvelian, Elamo-Dravidian, and Afro-Asiatic. This traces the main branches of the language evolutionary tree back in time, towards thicker boughs nearer the trunk.

The analysis focuses on certain core or fundamental words for basic concepts, such as small numbers (one, two), parts of body (eye, ear, foot, finger), important parts of the environment (tree, water) and pronouns (me, you). This is said to minimise the problems of borrowing, chance similarities, and cultural confusions. But some linguists say that it is a futile exercise. By the time languages are traced so far back in time, any root words and syntax are lost in the "static" of chance and random change.

THE NOSTRATES

Reconstructions of the supposed Nostratic language reveal many words for wild plants, but none for cultivated versions or farming techniques like planting. The words also show no differentiation between wild and domesticated animals, but throw up terms like haya –which roughly means running down game over a long period.

It is proposed that this language was spoken (by people called Nostrates) maybe 15,000 years ago. They were still hunter-gatherers – agriculture and animal husbandry had not yet developed. Such studies continue, and trace the development of languages as carriers of cultures, spread by farmers, warriors, merchants, and missionaries.

What about the main trunk of the language evolutionary tree? Could all languages have evolved from one original tongue, the spoken equivalent of Mitochondrial

(Below) A map based on dental evidence, showing how migrating human populations may have carried tooth patterns with them. The features of sundadonty (described in the text) appeared more than 20,000 years ago in southeastern Asia; the name comes from the Sunda Shelf, which was exposed around the present-day Indonesian islands by the lower sea levels of the time. The first people had reached Australia before sundadonty developed, which is why the early Australians had a more generalized "early modern" dental pattern. Then by 20,000–15,000 years ago, sinodonty appeared in the region of modern-day China. Bands of migrating humans took this pattern across the Bering Bridge to the Americas. Within the past few thousand years, sundadonts spread to the Pacific islands.

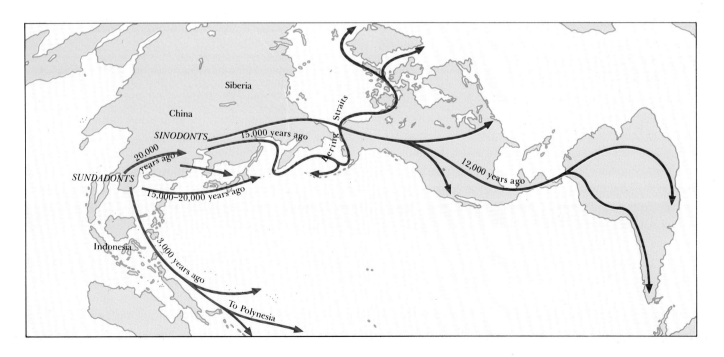

Eve, 100,000 or more years ago? This powerful notion is termed the "monogenesis of language." It is seen as an ultimate goal by some linguists, and as a waste of time and a great distraction by others.

AMERICAN LANGUAGES

Another very complex and controversial area in linguistics is New World languages. Tracing their origins could help to reveal when people first came to the Americas.

The 600-odd native American peoples languages have been variously grouped into about 155 families – or three. One of the three is Amerind, which includes many very different native American tongues. If the original Amerind language developed as people came to the New World, it should be about 12,000 years old, on archeological evidence such as the Clovis tools. However, extrapolating from language evolution in other continents, this is too short a time for the evolution of the present-day diversity of American languages. Analysis shows that a language family like Amerind, if it exists, should be 30,000–40,000 years old.

In the late 1980s, conclusions drawn from new (and controversial) evidence in linguistics, dental studies, and genetics and molecular biology, point to at least three separate waves of immigration from northeastern Asia into the New World. The first wave could have been as long ago as 60,000 years, or all three may have been relatively close together, beginning 20,000–15,000 years ago.

One group were Paleo-Indians, ancestors of some native North Americans and all native South Americans. They comprise the Amerind language family. Second came the Aleut-Eskimo group, who colonised the far northwest and northern coasts of North America, around to Greenland. They comprise the Aleut-Eskimo language family; they may have crossed the Bering land bridge around the same time as the Paleo-Indians, but along its southern rather than northern portion. The third wave of migrants, slightly later, gave rise to certain native American peoples groups in northwest and maybe southern central North America. They comprise the Na-Dene family of languages.

THE LAST 35,000 YEARS

The emergence of anatomically modern humans by 100,000 years ago is near the end of our story. But it is far from the end of the road to modern people. It was a full 65,000 years later before the first evidence for a "cultural explosion," involving blossoming tool technologies, art and self adornment, and eventually the abandoning of the hunter-gatherer way of life with the development of farming.

Traditionally this period began some 35,000 years ago, corresponding to the transition from Middle to Late (Upper) Paleolithic tool culture. The details of Stone Age tool developments are many and intricate, and some are described in the previous chapter. There

Above) The appearance of farming and herding practices typically marked the transition from the Mesolithic to the Neolithic (New Stone Age) phase. In parts of Europe this transition was occurring 9,000–6,000 years ago. This Neolithic village on the Orkney Islands, off northern Scotland, dates back 4,500 years. The excavation revealed the living floor of a house with a central stone hearth, and also stone shelves and resting areas.

was a gradation from the Upper Paleolithic tool culture of the Cro-Magnon people through the Mesolithic micro-blades (described below), to the development of Neolithic cultures with their ground and polished stone tools, and their domesticated animals and farmed crops.

Much of the evidence has focused on Europe, where the range and improvements in tools helped the people to survive harsh ice-age conditions. But new finds from other parts of the world are changing perceptions of Stone Age tool technologies. For instance, in southern

Above) Neolithic tools often show grinding and polishing. These English specimens include (from right to left) leaf-point arrowheads, a polished handaxe, a spearhead, and V-arrowheads.

PROTOLANGUAGES

Linguists working back into the past reconstruct root words of the various protolanguages, which have long since disappeared. They look for similarities and differences between two or a few languages, and analyse them to discover if both tongues are derived from a common ancestor. Pitfalls include the simple borrowing of words from another language, and onomatopaeic words whose sounds may mimic natural noises.

In the Indo-European group, the word father *in English has its equivalents as* vater *in German,* pater *in* Latin, *and* pitar *in Sanskrit. The reconstructed Indo-European root is* p'ter-. *This shows how "sound shifts" occur in the evolution of languages, and also – from the context of this term, in which the father is the head of a family – that patriarchal societies were present.*

The proto Indo-European language has several words for barley, wheat and other crops, and also for cows and other domesticated animals. The inference is that, when this language was being spoken, agriculture and animal husbandry were already developed.

Africa, advanced-looking tools which compare to the much later Upper Paleolithic stage in Europe, were already in use many thousands of years before their European counterparts. These Howiesons Poort tools, as the industries are known, include burins, blades, scrapers, and items shaped to fit into shafts, as composite tools. They are dated at about 70,000 years old.

PREHISTORIC ART AND ORNAMENT

What we call "art" – where an object's form and our appreciation of it take over from function – seems to have appeared relatively abruptly in human development, some 35,000 years ago. One of its earliest manifestations was body ornamentation, in which there was widespread indulgence by 30,000 years ago, in places as far apart as Europe and Australia.

These early objects, of a presumably symbolic rather

(left) Microliths are expertly chipped stone flake tools characteristic of the Mesolithic (Middle Stone Age) period. These are from Yorkshire, England.

than utilitarian nature, were beads and pendants, for body adornment. They were soon accompanied by early attempts to copy, represent or interpret animals and other significant aspects of the natural surroundings, either two-dimensionally in paintings and engravings, or three-dimensionally in sculptures and carvings.

Some of the earliest pendants and beads come from sites in Europe, and are dated at 34,000–30,000 years old. They are fashioned from a variety of materials, especially the ivory tusks of woolly mammoths, the teeth of other animals, and stones and shells. Many of these items are pierced by holes, presumably for hanging by cords on the body.

SCULPTURES AND PAINTINGS

It seems that three-dimensional sculptures and carvings were well developed 10,000 years before people began to paint or engrave sophisticated two-dimensional images. Many early sculptures from 30,000 years ago, of stone, bone, antler, and horn, represent animals. Some are decorated with puzzling patterns of crosses or lines, or grids of dots.

The materials for making these objects often originated at some distance from where they were found. In certain cases, the nearest available source is hundreds of miles away. Apparently the objects had enough significance to make this long-distance transport worthwhile. Another puzzle is that adornments and sculptures are very common at some archeological sites, yet rare or absent at otherwise comparable sites.

There are examples of rock art from Namibia, southwestern Africa, dating back about 27,000 years. By 25,000 years ago, early Australians were burying or cremating their dead, and using red ochre pigments for decoration; their art was relatively sophisticated by 20,000 years ago. The famous cave paintings such as those at Lascaux in France and Altamira in Spain date from less than 20,000 years ago.

WHY ART?

Why did people begin to expend time and effort in pleasing but apparently useless pursuits? Perhaps these activities had uses, other than the physical/manipulative functions filled by tools.

Body ornaments may have been worn to indicate social status within the group (like the stripes on the sleeves of today's armed forces). Many of the teeth, perforated for wearing on a cord, came from carnivorous animals such as the wolf, hyena, bear, and fox – symbols of strength, power and hunting success. A person without such an item was one of the crowd; the person wearing it was "somebody", like an individual of modern times wearing a visible sign of rank.

This indicates an ability to think in visual symbols. We are used to this now, in an age dominated by television, advertising images, and written words. It is difficult for us to imagine not thinking visually: that people may not have been able to mentally conjure up visual patterns, abstract from them certain qualities (like "sharpness" or "heaviness"), and place these qualities in new contexts or transfer them to new objects – as we do daily. This ability to think visually, manipulate images, and transfer qualities was important as art developed.

HUNTING MAGIC

Some paintings and sculptures may have been linked to the notions of magic, superstition, and ritual. Certain cave paintings seem to have "targets" added to the animals, or spears hitting the most effective part for a kill.

Were the images used for bringing good luck in the coming hunt – a kind of sympathetic hunting magic? Or did they fulfil a more prosaic function as target practice?

Lascaux in southwestern France, with its representations of deer, horses, and bulls, is the most extensively decorated cave of the period (Upper Paleolithic). Its paintings are 17,000 years old. Along with other examples of cave art, there are curious dots, lines, and curves both around and on the animals themselves – apparently, deliberately placed there by the artist. Various proposals suggest these indicated snares or traps, real or imaginary weapons, or symbols for males and females. Another suggestion, derived from a study of San (Bushman) and other art, is that the images were produced by hallucinating minds. Perhaps a shaman or "medicine man" went into a trance and, in an altered state of consciousness, produced the paintings as part of some ancient ritual.

(Right) The famous Venus of Willendorf (Austria), discovered in 1908, probably dates from 30,000-25,000 years ago and is an early example of statue art. The exaggerated female lines of this limestone figurine may have represented a "fertility goddess." Many such Venuses have been discovered in Soviet Asia, dating from about 25,000 years ago.

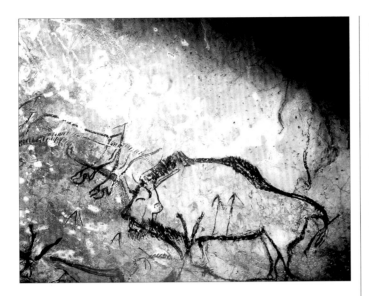

A bison wounded by arrows decorates the wall of the Grotte de Niaux, at Ariege in the French Pyrenees (left). It was painted towards the end of the Magdalenian culture (around 12,000-7,900 years ago). This time is generally regarded as a high point of Paleolithic art, and includes the famous cave paintings of Lascaux in France and Altamira in Spain. The Niaux paintings are over 1,640 feet (500 metres) from the cave's opening, so presumably they must have been executed by torchlight.

THE HUNTER-GATHERER LIFESTYLE

Farming and a more settled way of life originated in the Near East, perhaps 10,000–12,000 years ago. Wild grasses were planted and domesticated to become the first crops, and wild creatures such as sheep and goats were bred for animal husbandry. Yet farming was slow to spread to some regions, such as north-eastern Europe. New evidence suggests that the hunter-gatherer way of life, which people had followed for tens of millennia, was not the humble, haphazard business it may have seemed.

For example, in northern Eurasia, the last great Ice Age was waning by 10,000 years ago. "Postglacial foraging" took over for thousands of years in some areas, before agriculture spread slowly and erratically from the Near East. The Maglemosian people of eastern Britain and northern Europe were using microlith (small stone-flake) technology 9,000 years ago. They hunted deer, aurochs (a type of wild cattle, now extinct), wild pigs, hare, beaver, seals (near the coast), waterfowl, and fish. They harvested water chestnuts, hazelnuts and water lilies. They formed semi-permanent settlements, and stored food for lean seasons. Their hunter-gatherer lifestyle was highly successful, and ran parallel with nearby agriculture for thousands of years.

AND SO TO THE PRESENT

The search for our origins has come a long way since the discovery of the first Neandertal fossils in 1856. Old evidence is reinterpreted. Methods of excavation, analy-sis and dating progress. Surprises turn up. And basic questions are still discussed. Will the late Miocene gap be filled? Were any of the australopithecines our ancestors, or were they cousins? What of the variability of East African fossils from 2.5–1 million years ago, and what is the status of *Homo habilis*? Is *Homo erectus* our direct ancestor? When did speech evolve? Was there really an "African Eve"? How important were "key" events such as bipedality, using and making tools, communication and language, food sharing, cooperation and teamwork, use of fire, social systems, art and ceremony? Why are we so "successful"?

The past decades have produced many versions of the hominid family tree. Pendulums swing to and fro: lumpers and splitters, genes and bones, multi-regionalists and mono-regionalists. The fierce debate surrounding the quest for our past, with the preconceptions that it brings to light, perhaps tells us as much about ourselves as it does about our ancestors.

SITES, MUSEUMS, AND EXHIBITIONS

The fossils of prehistoric apes and humans are immensely valuable objects. In monetary terms, prized remains such as the original skeleton of Lucy, Skull 1470, and the Java skullcap are priceless. They confer great prestige on their discoverers and their guardians. And they are scientifically important because at any time they may be re-examined, re-measured and reassessed, in the light of new evidence and new perspectives on our past. For this reason, original fossils are often kept away from the public eye, in safety. The items on show in museums and exhibitions may well be plaster or fibre-glass casts of the originals, expertly treated and coloured to look like the real thing.

The sites of significant fossil finds are likewise valuable scientific assets. Sometimes their location remains a well-guarded secret, at least initially, to avoid damage by well-meaning but careless visitors, and to deter unscrupulous fossil-hunters. Some sites are open to the public as national monuments or places of special scientific interest. Opening hours may be restricted, perhaps seasonally, since staffing and security are costly. Public access to certain sites is very limited or non-existent, especially if excavations are continuing. However, a visit can sometimes be arranged by enquiring through the appropriate channels. This usually means contacting a museum, a university department, or a governmental department of science or antiquities.

MUSEUMS AND EXHIBITIONS

Most major natural-history and anthropology museums have information on human evolution, as do the smaller and more general provincial museums – especially if there has been an important find in the locality. Cities such as London (Natural History Museum and Museum of Mankind), Paris (Musée de l'Homme), New York (American Museum of Natural History), Chicago (Field Museum of Natural History), and Sydney (Australian Museum of Natural History) have exhibitions dedicated to displaying our past. Many of the unique African finds are housed at the National Museum of Kenya in Nairobi, the National Museum of Tanzania in Dar-es-Salaam, the National Museum of Ethiopia in Addis Ababa, and at museums and university departments throughout South Africa.

EUROPEAN SITES

Arago
Site location: Verdouble Valley, near the village of Tautavel 12 miles north-west of Perpignan, south-west France.
Principal finds: Skull parts from a *Homo erectus-Homo-sapiens* "protoneandertal" individual, depending on the interpretation.

La Chapelle-aux-Saints
Site location: Close to the village of La-Chapelle-aux-Saints, about 25 miles south-east of Brive, in the Dordogne region of France.
Principal finds: Skeleton of an adult male Neandertal individual.

Cro-Magnon
Site location: Cro-Magnon rock shelter, near the village of Les Eyzies, in the Dordogne region of France.
Principal finds: The original Cro-Magnon fossils, of anatomically modern humans *Homo sapiens sapiens.*

Heidelberg/Mauer
Site location: Rosch Sandpit, about half a mile north of Mauer village, approximately 6 miles south-east of Heidelberg, Germany.
Principal finds: A large lower jawbone, *Homo erectus-Homo sapiens.*

La Ferraise
Site location: About 2 miles north of Bugne, in the Dordogne region of France
Principal finds: Remains of several Neandertal individuals.

Neander Valley
Site location: Feldhofer Grotto cave on the slopes of the Neander Valley, near Hochdal, some 7 miles from Dusseldorf in the direction of Wuppertal, Germany. The cave, and most of the valley's side, has long since disappeared due to quarrying.
Principal finds: The original Neandertal remains.

Petralona
Site location: A cave near Petralona, 23 miles south-east of Thessalonika, east Greece.
Principal finds: Skull from a *Homo erectus-Homo sapiens* individual, depending on the interpretation.

Saint Cesaire
Site location: Pierrot's Rock, several hundred yards south of the village of Saint Cesaire, 7 miles from Saintes, in the Charente region, western France.
Principal finds: Parts of a Neandertal individual, the most recent remains yet discovered.

Steinheim
Site location: Sigrist Pit, Steinheim, 12 miles north of Stuttgart, Germany.
Principal finds: Skull parts from a *Homo erectus-Homo sapiens* "protoneandertal" individual, depending on the interpretation.

Swanscombe
Site location: Barnfield Pit, 2/3 mile south-west of All Saints Church, Swanscombe, Kent, England.
Principal finds: Skull parts from a *Homo erectus-Homo sapiens* "protoneandertal" individual depending on the interpretation.

Vértesszollos
Site location: Close to the village of Vértesszollos, 30 miles west of Budapest, Hungary.
Principal finds: Fragments of individuals of *Homo erectus-Homo sapiens*, depending on the interpretation.

NEAR EASTERN SITES

Amud
Site location: Wadi Amud, 6 miles north of Tiberias, Israel.
Principal finds: Skulls and other bones, broadly Neandertal.

Jebel Qafzeh
Site location: A cave on south-west Mount Qafzeh, about 1½ miles south of Nazareth, Israel.
Principal finds: Fossils of numerous individuals, broadly *Homo sapiens.*

Shanidar
Site location: Baradost Mountain, Shanidar Valley, 8 miles from the meeting of the Rowanduz and Greater Zab Rivers, about 250 miles north of Baghdad, Iraq.
Principal finds: Skulls and other bones of Neandertal-type individuals, plus burial and hearth evidence.

Skhul
Site location: Skhul Cave (Mughâret es-Skhul), a rock shelter some yards from the Tabun Cave
Principal finds: Skulls and other bones, probably of modern *Homo sapiens.*

Tabun
Site location: Tabun Cave (Mughâret et-Tabun), Wadi el-Mughara, western slopes of Mount Carmel, south-east of Haifa, Israel.
Principal finds: Skulls and other bones, probably of Neandertal-type individuals.

AFRICAN SITES

Border Cave
Site location: Border Cave, almost on the border between northern KwaZulu and Swaziland, 1 mile north of Ngwavuma Gorge, south-east Africa.
Principal finds: Early but probably anatomically modern *Homo sapiens* fossils.

Hadar
Site location: Near the Awash River, in the Afar Depression, some 190 miles north-east of Addis Ababa, Ethiopia.
Principal finds: Australopithecine and other fossils.

Koobi Fora (formerly East Rudolf)
Site location: The sites cover large area from Ileret south to Allia Bay, along the east shore of Lake Turkana, Kenya.
Principal finds: Australopithecine, habiline and *Homo erectus* remains.

Laetoli
Site location: On the southern Serengeti Plain, about 25 miles south of Olduvai (below), west of Ngorongoro Crater, Tanzania.
Principal finds: Fossil footprints, australopithecine fossils.

Makapansgat
Site location: Makapansgat Limeworks, 12 miles north-east of Potgieterus, Central Transvaal, South Africa.
Principal finds: *Australopithecus africanus* remains.

Olduvai
Site location: Main and Side Olduvai Gorge, Serengeti Plain, Tanzania, about 110 miles south-west of Nairobi, Kenya.
Principal finds: Many fossils of robust australopithecines, habilines and *Homo erectus.*

Omo
Site location: Many sites along the lower Omo River in Ethiopia, north of Lake Turkana.
Principal finds: Australopithecines and many other fossils.

Sterkfontein, Swartkrans, Kromdraai
Site location: These three cave-deposit sites are within a few miles of each other, about 5–7 miles north-west of Krugersdorp, South Africa.
Principal finds: Various australopithecine fossils.

Taung
Site location: Buxton Limeworks, 6 miles south-west of Taung, 80 miles north of Kimberley, South Africa.
Principal finds: The first-discovered australopithecine.

West Turkana
Site location: South bank of the Nariokotome River, near the west shore of Lake Turkana, Kenya.
Principal finds: Fossil skeleton of a *Homo erectus* youth.

FAR EASTERN SITES

Choukoutien (Peking Man)
Site location: Choukoutien (Choukoudian) cave, near the town of Zhoukoudian, 25 miles south-west of Beijing (Peking).
Principal finds: Peking-type *Homo erectus* fossils, tools and hearths.

Dali
Site location: Jiefang village, west Dali County, north of Xi'an (Sian), Shaanxi Province, China.
Principal finds: A *Homo erectus-Homo sapiens* skull.

Lantian
Site location: Two sites, Chenchiawo and Kungwangling Hill, in Lantian County, south of Xi'an (Sian), Shaanxi Province, China.
Principal finds: *Homo erectus* fossils.

Ngandong
Site location: 6 miles north of Ngawi, Java, Indonesia.
Principal finds: Many *Homo erectus* remains.

Sangiran
Site location: At the foot of the Lawu volcano by the Tjemoro River, near Surakarta, Java, Indonesia.
Principal finds: Many *Homo erectus* remains.

Trinil (Java Man)
Site location: Trinil, on the banks of the Solo River, 6 miles west of Ngawi, 19 miles north-west of Madium, Java, Indonesia.
Principal finds: The first recognised and other *Homo erectus* remains.

If you wish to see and learn more, these are the places to start. Look in the telephone book and in regional guidebooks, and enquire at local natural history and palaeontological societies (most large towns have them).

To arrange a special visit, in the first instance it is advisable to write to the information department, at the museum or other organisation in question.

Always check ahead before you make a visit. Some sites have no identification or facilities. Others may be closed for excavation or renovation. Opening hours vary with seasons and holiday periods – not to mention the wars and famines that afflict some regions.

GLOSSARY

Certain technical terms are used in different parts of the book. Their meanings are given here.

A

Absolute dating: a dating technique that can determine the age of a fossil or other remains in numbers of years since it was living.

Anatomy: The science of the structure of living things, including plants and animals.

Anthropoid: "apelike"; a member of the *Anthropoidea* (also known as *simians*), a suborder of the taxonomic order *Primates* which encompasses monkeys, apes, and humans.

Aboreal: tree-living.

B

Biology: the study of living things.

Bipedal: walks upright on two legs only.

Browsing: feeding above the ground on leaves and other plant matter in bushes and branches (compare *grazing*).

C

Canines: the long, pointed "eye teeth" between the *incisors* and the *cheek teeth*.

Carnivore: a meat-eater.

Cheek teeth: the *molars* and *premolars*, teeth behind the *canines* used for grinding or shredding food.

Clade: a natural group that contains all of the descendants of a common ancestor, and no other members. In biology, a clade can be any size of *taxon* (taxonomic group), from a *species* to an entire kingdom.

Cladistic analysis: a method of looking at relationships between groups. It involves the search for clades by – among other processes – identifying groups whose members possess certain features, termed shared derived characters or *synapomorphies*, which have been inherited from a common ancestor.

Cladogram: a branching treelike diagram, or other graphic representation, that depicts *clades* and how they are related to each other. A cladogram has no time scale, unlike a phylogeny.

Classification: a scheme that shows the relationships of groups of organisms.

Coprolite: fossilised faeces or excrement.

Cranium: the "brain-case," the rounded upper part of the skull that covers the brain.

Cusps: pointed cutting and grinding structures on mammalian *cheek teeth*.

D

Diastema: a gap between the *canine* tooth and the *cheek teeth*, often found in herbivorous mammals.

E

Enamel: the hard crystalline outer covering of a tooth. This is the hardest tissue in the body.

ESR: in *paleontology*, electron spin resonance. It is a method of *absolute dating* that involves changing the resonance or spin characteristics of electrons (particles within the atoms) of the material under study.

Extinction: death of a *species* or other *clade*.

F

Femur: thigh bone.

Fibula: the narrow shin bone running parallel to the *tibia*.

Foramen magnum: literally "big hole," the opening at the base of the skull through which the spinal cord passes from the brain down into the spinal column.

Fossilization: the processes of preservation of the remains of organisms in rocks.

G

Genus: the larger grouping into which a *species* is classified. For example, the genus *Homo* includes the species *Homo sapiens*, *Homo erectus*, and *Homo habilis*.

Glacial: pertaining to glaciers or glaciated episodes in the history of the Earth, which are sometimes loosely referred to as ice ages.

Grazing: feeding on grasses and other low vegetation (compare *browsing*).

H

Habitat: the physical and biological "place where an animal lives."

Herbivore: a plant-eater.

Hominid: a member of the group Hominidae, a taxonomic family of human and human-like apes. It includes all humans (living and extinct) of the *genus Homo* and their close relatives, the australopithecines.

Hominoid: a member of the group *Hominoidea,* a taxonomic superfamily. It includes all the *hominids* and all living and extinct apes (but not monkeys).

Humerus: the upper-arm bone.

I

Incisors: the front teeth, generally used for biting off food as opposed to tearing or chewing.

Interglacial: the warm spell between *glacials.*

L

Ligament: flexible tissues that join bones together around and within a joint.

M

Mandible: the lower jaw bone.

Maxilla: one of a pair of bones forming the upper jaw.

Molars: the *cheek teeth* at the back which are used for grinding or shredding food.

Morphology: the form and structure of an organism, in certain cases, as it is shaped by function.

N

Node: a branching point on a cladogram.

O

Occlusal: concerned with the grinding or biting surfaces of a tooth.

Omnivore: a creature that feeds on both plants and flesh.

Outgroup: in *cladistic analysis,* a separate "test group" against which the groups under study are compared.

P

Palaeoanthropology: the study of fossils or extinct *anthropoids,* the group which includes monkeys, apes, and (in this context most significantly) humans.

Palaeomagnetism: the study of how the Earth's magnetic field has changed in the past, from evidence "frozen" into rocks.

Palaeontology: the study of ancient life, usually restricted to the study of the fossil remains of prehistoric animals.

Parietal: pair of skull bones that form the skull roof.

Phylogeny: evolutionary relationships between groups of organisms, showing how they are related and the lines of ancestry and descent. The graphic representation is usually a branching diagram with a time scale – the "evolutionary tree" (compare *cladogram*).

Physiology: the study, extending to the level of molecules, of how plants and animals function.

Premolars: the front *cheek teeth,* just behind the canines. Premolars are not present in the milk (deciduous) dentition, only in the adult.

Primates: members of the Primates (pronounced "prime-ate-ees"), a major group (taxonomic order) within the mammals. It is usually divided into two subgroups, the *prosimians and the simians* (or *anthropoids).*

Prosimians: members of the *Prosimii,* a taxonomic suborder of the order *Primates.* It includes lemurs, lorises, bush babies, and tarsiers.

R

Radius: a bone of the forearm that runs parallel to the *ulna.*

Reconstruction: putting "flesh" on the bones of a fossil to convey how a creature may actually have looked.

Relative dating: a dating technique, also known as comparative dating, that shows whether a fossil or other remains is older or younger than another fossil, remains, or rock type.

Restoration: filling in the gaps in a damaged fossil to render it more complete.

S

Scapula: the shoulder blade.

Scavenger: an animal that feeds on dead plant or animal matter.

Sedimentary rock: a rock, such as mudstone, sandstone, or limestone, that formed from sediments laid down on land or under water.

Simians: one of the major divisions of the *primate* group, sometimes referred to as *Anthropoidea,* comprising monkeys, apes, and humans.

Skeleton: the hard parts of a body, which support and provide a framework for the soft parts. In humans and other mammals the internal skeleton is made of bones.

Species: a natural breeding group capable of producing like offspring.

Stratigraphy: the study of stratified rocks – those laid in layers, usually sedimentary rocks (the types that contain fossils).

Synapomorphy: "same new feature". In *cladistic analysis,* a shared, derived character or feature, which indicates that two groups are both descended from a common ancestor.

T

Taxon: a unit in *taxonomy,* from a species up to an entire kingdom. taxonomy: the scientific classification or grouping of living things.

Tendon: the tough connective tissue that attaches a muscle to a bone.

Tibia: the large shin bone that runs parallel to the *fibula.*

U

Ulna: a bone of the forearm that runs parallel to the *radius.*

V

Vertebra: a bone of the backbone or spinal column.

Vertebrate: an animal with vertebrae – a fish, amphibian, reptile, bird, or mammal.

Z

Zygomatic arch: the "cheek bone" –the bony arch beneath the eye socket.

INDEX

CREDITS

Quarto would like to thank the following for their help with this publication and for permission to reproduce copyright material.

Abbreviations: (a) above; (b) below; (l) left; (r) right; (t) top.

p7 (l) M. H. Day, (r) The Mansell Collection; **p8** John Reader; **p9** The Mary Evans Picture Library; **p10** The Mansell Collection; **p11** John Reader; **p12** The Mansell Collection; **p13** John Reader; **p17** L. Cowling/Trip; **p18** (t) Jeremy Draper/Trip, (b) Martin B. Withers/Frank Lane Picture Agency; **p19** Frank Lane Picture Agency; **p20** Fritz Polking/Frank Lane Picture Agency; **p21** (t) Frank Lane Picture Agency, (b) N. Dowe/Frank Lane Picture Agency; **p27** Eric and David Hosking/Frank Lane Picture Agency; **p28** Eric and David Hosking/Frank Lane Picture Agency; **p31** Silvestris/Frank Lane Picture Agency; **p34** John Tinning/Frank Lane Picture Agency; **p36** The Illustrated London News; **p37** The Illustrated London News; **p43** John Reader; **p45** Eric and David Hosking/Frank Lane Picture Agency; **p47** John Reader; **p48** University of Witwatersrand; **p49** Courtesy of the Department of Library Services/The American Museum of Natural History; **p50** (bl) University of Witwatersrand, (tr) Illustrated London News, (br) Illustrated London News; **p51** (tl) Illustrated London News, (bl) Illustrated London News; **p52** John Reader; **p53** M. H. Day; **p54** (tl) Frank Lane Picture Agency, (br) John Reader; **p56/57** John Reader; **p58** John Reader; **p60** M. H. Day; **p61** (tl) M. H. Day, (bl) M. H. Day, (r) John Reader; **p62** F. Fitch/GSF; **p63** M. H. Day; **p69** Martin B. Withers/Frank Lane Picture Agency; **p70** M. H. Day; **p71** M. H. Day; **p72** John Reader; **p73** M. H. Day; **p74** M. H. Day; **p75** (l) M. H. Day, (r) M. H. Day; **p76** (tr) C. M. Dixon, (tl) C. M. Dixon, (br) M. H. Day; **p83** John Reader; **p84** John Reader; **p85** Tony Waltham; **p86** (tl) C. M. Dixon, (tr) C. M. Dixon; **p87** (l) John Reader, (r) Illustrated London News; **p92** The Smithsonian Institute; **p94** C. M. Dixon; **p95** C. M. Dixon; **p102** (t) Helene Rogers/Trip, (b) M. H. Day; **p105** M. H. Day; **p108** M. H. Day; **p109** M. H. Day; **p111** John Reader; **p115** C. M. Dixon; **p116** C. M. Dixon; **p117** C. M. Dixon; **p120** Novosti Press; **p121** The Mansell Collection; **p122** C. M. Dixon; **p123** C. M. Dixon; **p129** Dave Saunders/Trip; **p131** Australian Overseas Information Service, London; **p132** Phil Ward/Frank Lane Picture Agency; **p134** C. M. Dixon; **p135** (t) C. M. Dixon, (b) C. M. Dixon; **p136** C. M. Dixon; **p137** C. M. Dixon.

Every effort has been made to trace and acknowledge all copyright holders. Quarto would like to apologise if any omissions have been made.